THE STORY OF VIỆT NAM

FROM PREHISTORY TO THE PRESENT

Key Issues in Asian Studies, No. 12

AAS Resources for Teaching About Asia

THE STORY OF VIỆT NAM

FROM PREHISTORY TO THE PRESENT

Association for Asian Studies, Inc.
825 Victors Way, Suite 310
Ann Arbor, MI 48108 USA
www.asian-studies.org

KEY ISSUES IN ASIAN STUDIES

A series edited by Lucien Ellington, University of Tennessee at Chattanooga

"Key Issues" volumes complement the Association for Asian Studies' teaching journal, *Education About Asia*—a practical teaching resource for secondary school, college, and university instructors, as well as an invaluable source of information for students, scholars, libraries, and those who have an interest in Asia.

Formed in 1941, the Association for Asian Studies (AAS)—the largest society of its kind, with over 8,000 members worldwide—is a scholarly, non-political, non-profit professional association open to all persons interested in Asia.

For further information, please visit www.asian-studies.org

For orders or inquiries, please contact:
Association for Asian Studies, Inc.
825 Victors Way, Suite 310
Ann Arbor, MI 48108 USA
Tel: (734) 665-2490
Fax: (734) 665-3801
www.asian-studies.org

Library of Congress Cataloging-in-Publication Data

Woods, L. Shelton, author.
The story of Viet Nam : from prehistory to the present / Shelton Woods.
    pages cm. — (Key issues in Asian studies ; no. 12) (AAS resources for teaching about Asia)
Includes bibliographical references.
ISBN 978-0-924304-71-2 (pbk. : alk. paper) 1. Vietnam—History. I. Title. II. Series: Key issues in Asian studies ; no. 12. III. Series: Resources for teaching about Asia.
  DS556.5.W65 2013
  959.7—dc23
                        2012047023

To Dirk Carlson
for your many years of friendship
for your care of Karen
for the many lives you bring into this world

and

To Brad Chaney
for your guidance
for your friendship
for the Hope that we share

ABOUT "KEY ISSUES IN ASIAN STUDIES"

Key Issues in Asian Studies (*KIAS*) volumes engage major cultural and historical themes in the Asian experience. *Key Issues* books complement the Association for Asian Studies' teaching journal, *Education About Asia*, and serve as vital educational materials that are both accessible and affordable for classroom use.

Key Issues books tackle broad subjects or major events in an introductory but compelling style appropriate for survey courses. Although authors of the series have distinguished themselves as scholars as well as teachers, the prose style employed is accessible for broad audiences. This series is particularly intended for teachers and undergraduates at two- and four-year colleges as well as advanced high school students and secondary school teachers engaged in teaching Asian studies in a comparative framework and anyone with an interest in Asia.

For further information about *Key Issues in Asian Studies*, *Education About Asia*, or the Association for Asian Studies, visit www.asian-studies.org.

Prospective authors interested in *Key Issues in Asian Studies* or *Education About Asia* are encouraged to contact:

> Lucien Ellington
> University of Tennessee at Chattanooga
> Tel: (423) 425-2118; E-Mail: Lucien-Ellington@utc.edu

"Key Issues" volumes available from AAS:

> *Modern Chinese History* by David Kenley
>
> *Korea in World History* by Donald N. Clark
>
> *Traditional China in Asian and World History* by Tansen Sen and Victor Mair
>
> *Zen Past and Present* by Eric Cunningham
>
> *Japan and Imperialism, 1853–1945* by James L. Huffman
>
> *Japanese Popular Culture and Globalization* by William M. Tsutsui
>
> *Global India circa 100 CE: South Asia in Early World History* by Richard H. Davis
>
> *Caste in India* by Diane Mines
>
> *Understanding East Asia's Economic "Miracles"* by Zhiqun Zhu
>
> *Political Rights in Post-Mao China* by Merle Goldman
>
> *Gender, Sexuality, and Body Politics in Modern Asia* by Michael Peletz

ABOUT THE AUTHOR

SHELTON WOODS is Professor of Southeast Asian History at Boise State University
where he also serves as the Associate Dean
in the College of Social Sciences and Public Affairs. He spent his first eighteen years
in Southeast Asia and moved to the United
States where he earned a PhD in Southeast
Asian History at the University of California,
Los Angeles. He is the author of four books:
Vietnam: An Illustrated History (New York:
Hippocrene, 2001); *A Broken Mirror: Protes-
tant Fundamentalism in the Philippines* (Ma-
nila: New Day Publishers, 2002); *Vietnam:
A Global Studies Handbook* (Santa Barbara:
ABC-CLIO, 2002); and *Japan: An Illustrated*
History (New York: Hippocrene, 2004). Dr. Woods's articles also appear in
various journals including: *Journal of Energy and Development*, *Philippine
Studies*, *Business Horizons*, and *Contemporary Southeast Asia*. He currently
lives in Boise where he is working on a biography of John Early, a former
governor of the Philippines' Mountain Province.

CONTENTS

ILLUSTRATIONS

Figures

Maps

Acknowledgments

While my name appears on the front of this booklet, it is only there because of the many people who have taught me in and outside of the classroom. These include John McMurrin, Rena Vassar, Ron Russell, Vince Ferguson, Valerie Matsumoto, Damodar Sardesai, Fred Notehelfer, and so many others who guided me into the world of history and writing. My parents sacrificed a great deal so I could learn from such distinguished mentors. A note to readers: it is best to express gratitude to your teachers while you have an opportunity to do so. I also wish to thank my students whose curiosity and passion for history make the classroom an oasis for me.

Lucien Ellington is a model editor and human being. His passion for history and the dissemination of Asian Studies across the United States is exemplary. His encouragement throughout the writing of this booklet was both reassuring and inspiring. We have worked together now for more than a decade, but after this project I consider him not only an advisor but also a friend. He is an amazing editor and I am thankful to know him. Lucien, my hope is that our best running days are still ahead of us. Thanks also to the anonymous readers who carefully read through each page of this volume and provided insightful feedback. Without Jonathan Wilson's help at the Association of Asian Studies, this work would not see the light of day. Thank you for your logistical help with regard to the manuscript, photos, and the overall production of the *Key Issues in Asian Studies* series. I have enjoyed our exchange of running and soccer stories. Jan Opdyke is a first-rate copyeditor, and I am humbled that this booklet is now part of the amazing portfolio of books that she has masterfully edited. Thank you so much for your careful reading of the manuscript.

A booklet seems an embarrassingly inadequate tribute to the countless number of people who have been part of Việt Nam's history. It is with deep-felt respect that this work is offered as a window into Việt Nam's past and present. Thank you to all those who have lived and died on behalf of what they hoped Việt Nam might become.

Finally, thank you to Lins and Karen. Lins, you are a source of indescribable joy and happiness to your parents. Thank you for your patience and instruction on our numerous fly-fishing expeditions. Karen, I can't come up with the words to say how thankful I am for you and how proud I am of you. This booklet and everything else I do is possible because of you. Thank you for the first twenty-five years and for the future.

Editor's Introduction

S helton Woods and I first worked together in 2001 when he did a superb job writing a longer book on Việt Nam for a series which I edited. Although Shelton's prior book was considerably different in scope than this *Key Issues* volume, it was also, like *Key Issues in Asian Studies*, intended for general readers. Shelton was the ideal editor's author in our first collaboration. He demonstrated a solid knowledge of content, a lucid and accessible prose style, reliability in meeting deadlines, and openness to suggestions. When we made the decision to develop a *Key Issues* volume on the history of Việt Nam, I immediately thought of Shelton and again, working with him has been a professional and personal pleasure.

Shelton, in a little over 80 pages of narrative, in my opinion, succeeds admirably in introducing Việt Nam's interesting and rich history. Thoughtful students who read this volume will never again think of Việt Nam as just another American war. Shelton provides students with excellent context for understanding Việt Nam's history and culture through his treatment of geography in the beginning of the volume. Although the subtitle of the book is "From Prehistory to the Present," Shelton manages to create succinct images in the reader's mind of Việt Nam's long relationship with China, its indigenous cultural history, and the impact of French colonialism. Yet he still devotes almost half the narrative to the post-World War II period. Students who finish the volume will have a basic understanding of the great achievements and possible perils of Việt Nam's recent economic rise and will also be positioned to reflect upon the nation's future problems and opportunities. The volume is suitable for a diverse array of survey courses ranging from human geography to world history.

As is the case with every *Key Issues* volume, a number of people worked hard in assisting in the book's development. Special thanks go to Thomas Gottschang who read the initial proposal and served as an external referee, as well as to Alan Whitehead, who also reviewed the manuscript. Thanks also go to Kitt McAuliffe, who is a University of Tennessee at Chattanooga honors student with an already deep interest in Asia. As an intern in our office, Kitt provided invaluable comments on various chapters of the volume. Finally, as always, I am deeply grateful to Jon Wilson, AAS Publications Manager, and to the AAS editorial board and especially to board chair Bill Tsutsui, for their unflagging support for pedagogical initiatives like *Education About Asia* and *Key Issues in Asian Studies*.

Lucien Ellington
Series Editor, Key Issues in Asian Studies

VIETNAMESE HISTORY
SIGNIFICANT EVENTS

2879–258 BCE	Legendary Hung dynasty
111 BCE	Việt Nam becomes part of China
40 CE	Trưng Trắc leads a revolt against China
42 CE	China successfully defeats Trưng Trắc and her supporters
544–602	Early Lý dynasty
938	Vietnamese defeat the Chinese navy at the Battle of Bạch Đằng River
1009–1225	Lý dynasty
1225–1400	Trần dynasty
1287	Mongols withdraw from Việt Nam
1371	Cham army captures Thăng Long, the capital of the Trần state
1407–28	Việt Nam is incorporated into China's Ming empire
1428–1780	Lê dynasty
1550–1600	Portugal and Spain create colonies in Southeast Asia
1600–1770	Trịnh and Nguyễn clans rule behind the scenes
1771–1802	Tây Sơn brothers fight for control of Việt Nam
1802–1945	Nguyễn dynasty
1807	Gia Long reinstates the Confucian-based civil service examination system
1825	Emperor Minh Mạng forbids the practice of Christianity in Việt Nam
1858	French attack and occupy Đà Nẵng
1862	Treaty of Sài Gòn gives France Gia Định and three surrounding provinces

1885	Emperor Thuyết calls on the Vietnamese to expel the French from Việt Nam
1887	France creates the Indochina Union
1890	Hồ Chí Minh is born
1911–41	Hồ Chí Minh travels, works, and studies outside of Việt Nam
1912	Assassination attempt on Governor General Sarraut
1919	At the Paris Peace Conference, Vietnamese unsuccessfully seek independence from France
1925	Hồ helps found the Communist Youth League
1927	Vietnamese Nationalist Party (VNQDD) is founded
1930	VNQDD fails in leading a general uprising against French rule
1930	Indochinese Communist Party founded
1940	Japanese occupy northern Việt Nam
1941	Japanese occupy southern Việt Nam
1941	Việt Nam Độc Lập Đồng Minh Hội (Việt Minh) is founded
1945	Hồ Chí Minh declares the independence of Việt Nam
1946–1954	First Việt Nam War
1954	Geneva Conference divides Việt Nam at the seventeenth parallel (Democratic Republic of Việt Nam (DRV) in the north and Republic of Việt Nam (RVN) in the south)
1955	Ngô Đình Diệm, with support from the United States, wins the RVN political election
1960	Lê Duẩn is elected secretary of the Vietnamese Communist Party
1963	Ngô Đình Diệm and Ngô Đình Nhu are assassinated
1964	Tonkin Gulf Resolution is passed by the US Congress
1965	President Johnson orders American troops into Việt Nam
1968	Tết Offensive leads many Americans to question the US involvement in Việt Nam

1969	Hồ Chí Minh dies
1973	Paris Peace Accords establish a cease-fire and withdrawal of US troops from Việt Nam
1975	Republic of Việt Nam falls to the Democratic Republic of Vietnam
1976	A united Việt Nam becomes known as the Socialist Republic of Việt Nam
1978	Việt Nam invades and occupies Cambodia
1979	China invades northern Việt Nam and fierce battles are fought north of Hà Nội
1986	Implementation of economic renovation in Việt Nam
1988	Việt Nam's Politburo issues Resolution 10, which ends the widespread use of collectivization of land and labor
1989	Vietnamese troops withdraw from Cambodia after a ten-year occupation
1990–2000	Việt Nam is the world's second-fastest-growing economy
1995	Normalization of US–Việt Nam Relations
2007	Việt Nam joins the World Trade Organization
2012	Việt Nam passes a law claiming sovereignty over the Paracel and Spratly Islands

The Socialist Republic of Việt Nam. (Courtesy of the University of Texas
Libraries, University of Texas at Austin.)

INTRODUCTION

E veryone enjoys an exciting story. No matter how dramatically technology changes our daily lives, we still love to watch, hear, and read exciting tales. It is hard to find a story more compelling than that of Việt Nam. It is a gripping narrative full of twists and turns, including centuries of expansion and war and an abiding passion for liberty.

In particular, the story of Việt Nam is intertwined with today's three largest economies: those of the United States, China, and Japan. China ruled Việt Nam for more than a thousand years, and as recently as 1979 the two nations fought a brief war. Japan's occupation of southern Việt Nam in July 1941 led to US sanctions. Japan responded with the bombing of Pearl Harbor on December 7, 1941, setting off World War II in the Pacific.

America is connected to Việt Nam. While an immense ocean separates the two countries, their histories are forever interwoven with the threads of blood, tears, laughter, misunderstanding, and reconciliation. As part of the *Key Issues in Asian Studies* series, this volume unlocks multiple doors to our understanding of both the United States and Việt Nam. It is easy to make a case for why Americans should take an interest in Việt Nam.

"This is not going to be another Vietnam." This sentence, uttered many times by American officials, is just one example of how important Việt Nam is to our past and present. Since the 1975 fall of South Việt Nam, important aspects of American foreign policy have fundamentally changed. From the latter nineteenth century until 1975, Americans appeared invincible. Their unreserved optimism was rooted in taming the frontier, keeping the union together despite the Civil War, and a perfect record of victories in foreign wars. In 1898, after America's quick victory over Spain, President William McKinley decided to extend his nation's rule to Asia and took the Philippines away from Spain, making it an American colony. But just a half century later, Việt Nam crushed Americans' notion of being perpetual winners. Despite being the planet's greatest economic and military power during the 1960s, the United States could not defeat the North Vietnamese.

More than sixty thousand Americans paid the ultimate price for their country during the Việt Nam War. More than ten times that number of Vietnamese perished during the war. The brutal conflict not only claimed so many lives but it also destroyed much of Việt Nam's environment and economy. But while economies might rebound, some broken lives need more than a lifetime to heal. American soldiers who returned to the United States after serving in the war found themselves haunted by demons of the past and despised by many of their own citizens who opposed the war.

The war divided the United States. The antiestablishment, civil rights, free love, and hippie movements of the 1960s latched onto Việt Nam as a symbol of everything that was wrong with the United States. The war so rooted itself in American culture that many folk and popular songs were written about the war, including "Fortunate Son," "Masters of War," "Born in the USA," "The Fightin' Side of Me," and "Ohio." Hollywood was also profoundly affected as it distributed scores of movies related to the war, including "The Deer Hunter," "Platoon," "Born on the Fourth of July," "The Quiet American," "We Were Soldiers," and "Good Morning Vietnam." The Việt Nam War affected American literary culture as well, with novels, histories, and memoirs written about the war, including *A Bright Shining Lie, Fire in the Lake, The Things they Carried, The Best and the Brightest,* and *A Rumor of War.*

For the American generations that have come of age since the war, Việt Nam is more relevant because of the numerous Vietnamese who have made America their home. In terms of Asian immigrants, the Vietnamese are latecomers to the shores of the United States. After the 1975 conclusion of the Việt Nam War, large numbers of Vietnamese made their way to the United States through asylum requests and dangerous voyages that often involved first reaching other Asian countries. In 2012 there were close to two million Vietnamese Americans, making them the fourth largest Asian American group in the country. Many Vietnamese came to the United States with nothing but emotional and mental scars from the war, and yet they have flourished here. The long list of Vietnamese Americans who have risen in their respective fields stretches from Texas state representative Hubert Vo to former Dallas Cowboys' linebacker Dat Nguyen. Vietnamese restaurants throughout the United States also demonstrate the integration of these two cultures.

Finally, Americans should be keenly interested in Việt Nam because of the growing critical role of the U.S. military in the Pacific. China's growing influence in Asia is backed by its dynamic economy and rapidly expanding military. To protect its interests in Asia, the United States will need to cultivate friendships and partnerships. Việt Nam is a perfect ally. While it stubbornly holds onto its authoritarian-style government, it has become one of the world's brightest spots for international businesses. The ensuing chapters chronicle Việt Nam's sweet and sour relationship with China, and it would benefit by partnering with the United States as both seek a balance of power in Asia rather than a dominant Chinese influence.

The following pages tell the story of Việt Nam from a broad perspective. Covering three thousand years in a brief volume is a challenge for both the writer and the reader. But this book is meant to be a beginning, not an end—a general narrative that provides a solid understanding of Việt Nam's troubled yet inspiring journey. If the longest journey begins with a first step, reading the following pages needs to be our first step in learning how much Việt Nam might teach us about the human spirit.

1

Prehistory to 100 BCE

We don't get to choose where and when we are born, our biological parents, or whether we enter the world healthy or ill. As we begin our exploration of Việt Nam it is helpful to remember that millions of people, through no choice of their own, entered this planet in Việt Nam. But while the Vietnamese, like the rest of us, had no say as to their birthplace, they consciously created a society rooted in their love of life and freedom. The Vietnamese people's deep-seated commitment to life and liberty has been severely tested over the years. One of the many examples of these struggles is clearly seen in the following statistic: within the last century the three countries with the world's largest economies, the United States, China, and Japan, all attempted to impose their political ideologies on the Vietnamese by military means. Many paid the ultimate price because their leaders underestimated the strength and depth of Vietnamese culture. If we could call on Việt Nam's soil to serve as a witness to the numerous battles that solidified Vietnamese culture, it might claim to have performed its role as the repository for the blood and tears of both soldiers and civilians. But the ground would also claim that it has witnessed countless days of peace and joy among those privileged to call Việt Nam their home.

Beginning Stories

Myths often contain strands of historical reality shrouded in fables. Hence, though Việt Nam's earliest history comes down to us in the form of fantastic superhero stories, actual events helped shape these stories passed down via oral tradition. The legend of Việt Nam's beginning centers on the sea meeting the mountains. A quick glance at a map helps explain this story. Shaped like an S and sitting at the eastern edge of mainland Southeast Asia, Việt Nam's total land area (203,980 square miles) make it slightly smaller than New Mexico. Mountains define most of the country's topography and less than one fourth of the land is level. While the length

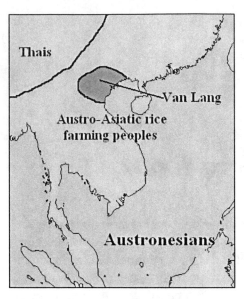

Map 1.1. The earliest Vietnamese state, also known as Van Lăng. It emerged in the north near the Chinese border. (Courtesy of Briangotts, http://commons. wikimedia.org/wiki/File:World_500_ BCE_showing_Van_Lang.png.)

of Việt Nam (north to south) is 1,023 miles, its many inlets and its protrusion into the South China Sea give it a coastline of just over 2,000 miles. The earliest people groups that merged to form a Vietnamese identity were the linguistic Austronesian family from the islands of Southeast Asia. Then, around 3,000 BCE families in southern China began moving south into Việt Nam's northern mountains. The 1,860 square mile fertile Red River delta proved to be the perfect Petri dish for the mixture of these groups. But ancient legends tell us that Việt Nam's birth came with great travail.

The best-known version of Việt Nam's origin story tells of the fear that haunted the clans in the Red River delta because of invading northern peoples. It is probable that this legend references the Austronesian people of the lowlands who faced the threat of a more sophisticated and powerful people moving into the area from China. Then, coming from the east and out of the water, a dragon/superhero named Lạc Long Quân reportedly defended the delta-dwelling people and in the process captured and married Âu Cơ, the invading king's wife. Together they parented a hundred children; half of them returned to the waters with their father, while the other half remained on the land, continuing to populate the Red River delta.

This story describes the Vietnamese as a people whose origins derive from both the eastern sea and the northern mountains. It also reveals how the first Vietnamese communities developed along the fertile soil of the Red River delta. In addition, these origin stories square with the linguistic history of the Vietnamese: the foundation of their language was from the Austro-Asiatic family while they also heavily borrowed vocabulary from Chinese.

The Lạc Long Quân tale correctly indicates that the origins of Việt Nam were in its northern regions. It was only in the past few centuries

6

that the Vietnamese expanded their border south through migration and military conquests. As one expert on Việt Nam's past writes, "'[T]raditional' Vietnam refers primarily to the Red River delta and the central coastal plains regions, mainly as they existed in the nineteenth century."[1] Eventually, northern, central, and southern Việt Nam became identified with three major urban centers.

Figure 1.1. Rice, historically the foundation of Việt Nam's economy. Rice often served as the basis of taxation and tribute paid to overlords. (Courtesy of Wikimedia Commons http://commons.wikimedia. org/wiki/File:Vietnampaddyrice.jpg.)

Hà Nội is the northern city identified with the country's earliest cultural and social centers; the central city of Hué became the imperial capital as the emperors used this geographical middle ground to balance the competing interests of powerful northern and southern clans; and Hồ Chí Minh City, once known as Sài Gòn, was the frontier city where risk-taking entrepreneurs found a place in Việt Nam's southern Mekong delta.

For communities to form and stay in one area there must be enough food. In northern Việt Nam, there wasn't sufficient game for hunters and gatherers to survive. Moreover, brutal yearly typhoons made fishing merely a seasonal occupation. The solution was rice. Ancient self-sustaining societies along the Red River delta flourished because of rice. While some histories are observed through the lens of dates and names, Việt Nam's history was profoundly shaped by rice. This is because most Vietnamese spent their days laboring in rice paddies. Only a small percentage of the population influenced Việt Nam's political history; so, to understand what occupied most of the ancient Vietnamese, we must turn to rice.

Combining the story of Lạc Long Quân and the role of rice, the Vietnamese ancient legend asserts that one of his offspring was the first king of the Hung dynasty (2879–258 BCE). During this era, cultivation of rice resulted in the emergence of small estates consisting of paddies called Lac fields. Proprietors of these agricultural lands became known as Lac lords and formed a loose confederation of powerful leaders.

Three things about rice help explain how landowners emerged from this agrarian-based economy. First, rice farming is incredibly labor intensive because it entails constructing and maintaining paddies, monitoring water levels—usually through the use of sophisticated irrigation systems—and the tedious work of planting, harvesting, and husking the grain. All of this work creates community, as it takes cooperation among many to build paddies and do the work necessary to ensure a bountiful rice harvest. A common agrarian need to survive united the early Vietnamese communities. Finding political protection under the hegemonic overview of the Lac lords allowed Vietnamese farmers to concentrate on the seasonal tasks connected with rice farming. Second, farming rice consumed the lives of early Vietnamese because they knew that rice contains enough nutrients to sustain life, especially if a little salt is part of the overall diet. Rice equaled security. Given the rich soil of the Red River delta, the rice farmers didn't have to look further than the soil they tilled for tomorrow's food. Finally, rice was so important because it could be stored. Unlike fish, animal meat, or leafy vegetables, rice could be kept and consumed months—if not years—after harvest. This also meant that rice could be used as the basis of a tax paid by the peasants to the dominant landowner in their area. The individual with the most rice could also afford the largest protection force to control the best farmland. Eventually, poor landless farmers were drawn to private Lac fields. Quid pro quo relationships developed in which poor farmers provided labor to Lac lords in exchange for economic and physical protection.

EARLY POLITICAL STATES IN VIỆT NAM
VĂN-LANG, ÂU LẠC, AND NAN YÜEH

The rulers of the Hung dynasty reportedly named their kingdom "Văn-lang." This state existed during the first millennium BCE during what archaeologists call the Dong-son culture. A distinctive feature of this society was the use of bronze, which points to a degree of complexity, as producing bronze allowed for better tools, weapons, and especially drums used in religious ceremonies. There is also evidence that Văn-lang peoples domesticated water buffaloes for use in plowing rice paddies. The increased technological sophistication of the Vietnamese spread to other parts of Southeast Asia, which indicates migration and trade between the earliest Vietnamese states and other parts of Asia.

As centuries passed, a center of power emerged in the Red River plain that Lac lords acknowledged through voluntary payment of tribute. It would take a relatively significant center of power to produce bronze and

Văn-lang, 2879– 258 BCE (ruled by mythical Hung kings)

Âu Lạc, 257–207 BCE (established by An Duong,
a Chinese intruder and the first historical figure
in Việt Nam's history)

Nan Yüeh, 207–111 BCE (Established by Chao-T'o,
Việt Nam became part of an independent southern China
state called Nan Yüeh. Việt Nam encompassed the two
Nan Yüeh provinces of Giao-Chỉ and Cuử-chân.)

Chiao-chi Circuit, 111 BCE–938 CE (Việt Nam became
part of Han China's Chiao-chi Circuit. It encompassed
three of Chiao-chi's seven prefectures:
Giao-Chỉ, Cuử-chân, and Nhất Nam)

Figure 1.2. Việt Nam's evolving early states.

serve as the religious capital for the region. But rumblings in the north
shook the established patterns in Việt Nam, which moves us from the
realm of legend to history.

Van Lăng and its Hung kings were overthrown in approximately 257
BCE by an invading official from China named An Duong, who established
a new state called Âu Lạc. While An Duong is the first verifiable historical
figure in Việt Nam, a great deal of myth surrounds the secret of his victory
over the Hung king. A golden turtle from the sea is said to have invited
An Duong to remove one of its claws, which he used to make a bow that
could simultaneously shoot thousands of arrows. With this weapon, An
Duong became the king of Việt Nam and built its capital at Cỗ Loa, on the
outskirts of today's Hà Nội.

Âu Lạc was destined to be a short-lived entity. While King An Duong
consolidated his state, the numerous states of China surrendered to the

Figure 1.3. Ceremonial helmet from the Trần dynasty around the year 1150 CE. Compared to the rest of Southeast Asia, Việt Nam was an early adapter of bronze. (Courtesy of Prodvocalist, http://commons.wikimedia.org/wiki/File:Bronze_ceremonial_helmet_from_the_Tran_Dynasty_in_Dai-Viet_%28modern-day_Vietnam%29_circa_12th_-_13th_century.JPG.)

Qin state, led by King Shihuang-di who became the first emperor of a united China: the Qin empire (221–206 BCE). However, following the rapid collapse of the Qin (Chinese scholars claimed that the dynasty lasted less than two decades because its leaders eschewed philosophy in favor of harsh rule), Chao-T'o, a Chinese official based in the southern Chinese city of Guangzho, raised the banner of independence, took control of China's southern state of Nan Yüeh, and extended this new state farther south at the expense of Âu Lạc. At the time, An Duong still ruled Âu Lạc. Oral tradition claims that when Chao-T'o attacked Âu Lạc he somehow stole the bow of the turtle's claw and overran the capital, Cỗ Loa, incorporating Việt Nam into Nan Yüeh. Once Chao-T'o conquered all of Cỗ Loa, he divided it into two prefectures: Giao-chỉ and Cuử-chân. This represented an unprecedented, but soon recurring, pattern of Việt Nam's subjection to a much larger northern entity.

But the independent Nan Yüeh would also be a short-lived state due to the rise of the much stronger Chinese Han dynasty (206 BCE–220 CE). The Han lasted longer than the Qin dynasty because it incorporated the strong legalistic aspects of the Qin empire and the philosophical teachings of past sages. When in 111 BCE the Han brought Nan Yüeh into its empire, Han officials changed the designation of Nan Yüeh to the Chiao-chi Circuit. This consisted of seven prefectures, three of which made up the Việt Nam area: the existing Giao-chỉ and Cuử-chân prefectures and the newly created Nhất Nam area. Census data from the first years of the Common Era indicate that 72 percent of the households in Chiao-chi were located in modern Việt Nam. The dust from the political chaos finally settled a hundred years before the Common Era, and Việt Nam was integrated into China's empire. It would be politically attached to its northern neighbor for the next thousand years.

2

EARLY OUTSIDE INFLUENCES
(100 BCE TO 400 CE)

A quick glance at Việt Nam's political scene between 300 and 100 BCE can be confusing given the number of governmental transitions. From Văn-lang to Âu Lạc to Nan Yüeh, Việt Nam eventually became part of the Han Circuit of Chiao-chi. But in 100 BCE, once the Han armies incorporated Việt Nam into the Chinese empire, the relationship between Việt Nam and China was established—a workable arrangement that lasted a thousand years. It was far from a perfect system, but longevity is proof of stability. Yet, despite Chinese influence, scores of generations developed a distinctive culture that took root in the hearts and lives of the Vietnamese.

SINO-VIETNAMESE INTERACTION

When the Chinese invading generals entered Việt Nam in 100 BCE, they acknowledged that the influence of indigenous Lac lords was an effective means of governing the many farmers in the Red and Ma river plains. So why fix what isn't broken? The only change the Chinese made to this economic system was that instead of the Lac lords paying tribute to the deposed Vietnamese kings, they were told to pay taxes to the Han-appointed provincial governor. Lac lords readily switched allegiances to the victorious Han generals and China-appointed officials because the Chinese allowed them to maintain their economic and social positions. However, the Chinese did insist that the Lac lords recognize the new territorial boundaries placed on Việt Nam. The Chinese-imposed boundaries had no effect on the Lac lords' landownership, and Han officials legitimized the position of the Lac lords by providing them with visible tokens of authority, such as ribbons and seals. The Lac lords retained their lands, received external validation, and became economic allies of the massive Han empire. But the downside to their new relationship with China was that they were now dependent on a foreign entity to authenticate their heretofore assumed status. Given this new relationship with Chinese officials, the Lac lords had only two options: dance to the tune of the Han bureaucrats or declare independence—which meant war.

Map 2.1. Southeast Asia. Because of its geographic position, Việt Nam experienced a great deal of interaction with East, South, and Southeast Asia from its earliest history. (Courtesy of the University of Texas Libraries, University of Texas at Austin.)

For more than a century, relative peace characterized relations between the Vietnamese and the Chinese, but two major factors worked against what had been an amiable partnership. The fertile soil of Việt Nam attracted many Chinese families, some of which had the means to compete economically with indigenous proprietors. Also, Lac lords complained that Chinese officials were steadily increasing their tax demands to unreasonable levels. In the spring of 40 CE Trưng Trắc, the wife of a beleaguered Lac lord, led a successful revolt against Chinese rule. She attracted indigenous support by promising that levels of tribute would become reasonable and that the pre-Han system would return for the Vietnamese. With help from her sister, Trưng Nhị, Trưng Trắc fulfilled her vow to her allies. Unfortunately their military and economic victories over the Chinese did not last long.

A brilliant Han general, Ma Yuan, along with twenty thousand troops, firmly reestablished Chinese control over Việt Nam. Some historical records indicate that the Trưng sisters were captured and their heads sent to the Han emperor; other documents claim that the sisters committed suicide rather than surrender. An important legacy of this revolt is that future Vietnamese revolutions were not exclusively the work of adult men, but all segments of society were called to emulate the bravery and sacrifice of the Trưng women.

Following his victory, Ma Yuan correctly surmised that continued Chinese rule in the three southern prefectures would be much easier if some of his Han soldiers were to settle in Việt Nam. Prior to Ma Yuan's victory, the Chinese in Việt Nam were usually high-class migrants whose families had lost their positions—usually for backing the losing side in political battles—who had fled south to hold on to their possessions. These early Chinese in Việt Nam are best characterized as visitors rather than settlers. They had little if any interest in the Vietnamese people; their ultimate goal was to return to "civilization" when things calmed down in China, which was just emerging from a period of multiple civil wars. But Ma Yuan's soldiers were different. While they did not possess the wealth or sophistication of earlier Chinese, the soldiers were more likely to make a life for themselves in Việt Nam. Their general gave them conquered lands, and many married Vietnamese women, creating a new group of individuals that became known as Han-Việt families. These groups' social connections through marriage helped pave the way for Việt Nam's political integration into China.

CONFUCIANISM AND VIỆT NAM

Việt Nam's annexation into the Han polity coincided with the growth of Confucian thought in the empire. This philosophy was rooted in the five Chinese Classics (the *Book of Changes*, *Spring and Autumn Annals*, *Book of Rites*, *Book of Songs*, and *Book of Documents*), which focused on poetry, history, ritual, and divination, along with the Four Great Books (*The Confucian Analects, The Mencius, The Doctrine of the Mean*, and *The Great Learning*). A primary goal of Confucian philosophy is to nurture

Figure 2.1. An altar in Nha Trang, Việt Nam. While Việt Nam accepted religions from foreign lands, there was an indigenous animist-based faith that included the worship of unseen powers. (Courtesy of Dragfyre, http://commons.wikimedia.org/wiki/File:Altar_at_Po_Nagar.jpg.)

a peaceful society based on a virtuous populace. It starts with each individual following proper ritual protocols and filling one's role in the web of human relationships, whether as a leader or a subordinate.

One prejudice of Confucianism was its assumption that those ignorant of Chinese philosophy, art, and literature were inferior. Another group that it discriminated against was women. So when Chinese officials began to integrate Confucianism into Vietnamese society, they did so with the presupposition that the local culture was inferior and needed to change. They did this in part because they insisted on viewing all societies through the lens of their own categories. One historian notes, "Chinese sources tended to assume that their neighbors in Southeast Asia, which they usually classified as vassals of China, were essentially small replicas of China."[1] However, the Chinese did regard members of the Vietnamese literati, who were steeped in Confucian learning, as philosophical brothers, according them high social status in both Việt Nam and China.

The imposition of the Confucian worldview on the Vietnamese extended to relations between men and women. Han officials were disgusted that the Vietnamese didn't have "proper" notions of marriage. And even after three hundred years of Chinese rule, a local Han administrator wrote, "In Nhatnam Prefecture, men and women go naked without shame. In short, it can be said that these people are on the same level as bugs."[2]

These harsh assessments of Vietnamese society are somewhat attributable to basic Sino-Vietnamese differences in family relations.

Women were accorded greater rights in Việt Nam—and this pattern continued despite a thousand years of Chinese rule. Nonetheless, the Chinese tenaciously tried to make over the Vietnamese in their image. For example, in the first century a Han-appointed official insisted that Vietnamese men and women marry in a Chinese-style wedding ceremony, with Lac lords providing the needed funds for ceremonial expenses. Such policies characterized Chinese rule in Việt Nam. But in some ways Việt Nam during Chinese rule was like a sponge that mixed Chinese customs with indigenous practices. Việt Nam might have discriminately absorbed aspects of the Chinese worldview, but it still remained a sponge. Another scholar put it this way: "The Vietnamese language survived, and it is reasonable to assume that after the first or second generation Han immigrants spoke Vietnamese. Vietnamese society as a whole remained separate from Chinese civilization, and Han-Viet society existed as a wing of this autonomous cultural world. Han immigrants were more effectively 'Vietnamized' than the Vietnamese were sinicized [to adopt Chinese culture]."[3]

BUDDHISM IN VIỆT NAM

Another external influence on Việt Nam that occurred about the same time as Ma Yuan's invasion was Buddhism. It is probable that Buddhism arrived in Việt Nam before it made its way to China. This world religion began in northern India during the sixth century BCE, and it stood in contrast to the dizzyingly complex and hierarchical world of Brahmanism, which defined India's religious landscape at the time.

Founded by Prince Siddhartha Gautama, the basic doctrine of Buddhism is that selfish human desire gives birth to pain

Figure 2.2. Statue of the Bodhisattva of Mercy found near Đà Nẵng, Việt Nam. Buddhism introduced new art forms into Việt Nam. (Courtesy of CE photo, Uwe Aranas, http://commons.wikimedia.org/wiki/File:67-meter-high_statue_of_the_Bodhisattva_of_Mercy_on_Son_Tra_Peninsula.jpg.)

15

and suffering along with rebirth. To relieve suffering and a continual return to this world of pain, an individual must renounce his or her selfish desires and follow a path of action motivated by selflessness, benevolence, and compassion.

Following the Buddha's death (Siddhartha became the Buddha after his earthly enlightenment), a canon of Buddhist sacred texts emerged along with the Sangha, communities of faith committed to the Buddha's teaching.

One dominant branch of Buddhism, known as Mahayana, was zealously mission minded. Its adherents believed that one of the greatest acts of selflessness one could undertake was moving to a foreign land to spread the Buddhist faith. And so Buddhist monks came to Việt Nam. By the time of the Common Era, ports along Giao-chi bustled with trade, bringing goods from the rest of Southeast Asia and India. South Asian monks traveled to Việt Nam via ships with their merchant friends. While some claim to know the exact date on which the first Buddhist missionary arrived on Việt Nam's shores, it is safer to say that Buddhism arrived in Việt Nam around the beginning of the Common Era.

Buddhism offered the Vietnamese all the trappings of a world religion: sacred texts, a clergy, elaborate ceremonies, and breathtaking art and architecture. But as this foreign faith took root there, it did so with a very local flavor. For example, Luy-lâu, the political center of Việt Nam during the third century CE also became the epicenter of Buddhism, with over twenty temples and five hundred monks. Four of the earliest Buddhist temples in Luy-lâu were devoted to the Buddha of Clouds, Rain, Thunder, and Lightning (devastating typhoons annually cause havoc in the region). A pantheon of deities in the Vietnamese spiritual world predated the arrival of Buddhism. Just as the Chinese influence in Việt Nam was truly "Vietnamized," so, too, was Buddhism Vietnamized by the locals' preexisting faith. Nonetheless, the appealing aspects of Buddhism seemed to attract all classes of Vietnamese. But, like other world religions, Buddhism's influence eventually turned political and Buddhists played a role in spurring rebellions that eventually led to Việt Nam's independence from China.

Both Confucianism and Buddhism helped shape Vietnamese culture, but as a writer once noted, the outside influences on Southeast Asia were just a "thin, flaking glaze" underneath which was the real cultural foundation based on indigenous values.[4] For example, both Mahayana Buddhism and Confucianism address the nature of political and metaphysical power. Although the Vietnamese incorporated these foreign

16

Figure 2.3. Monks walking in the morning in Da Lat, Việt Nam. Buddhism
remains the dominant religion in the country. (Courtesy of Diane Selwyn,
http://commons.wikimedia.org/wiki/File:Monks_in_the_Morning,_Da_Lat.jpg.)

ideas, their functional belief was that the cosmos was animated by unseen
energy, malevolent and benevolent gods, and their ancestors' ghosts.
These unseen powers affected every aspect of life to the point that regular
ritual rites provided the deference, respect, and offerings the Vietnamese
believed were appropriate, if not demanded, for these unseen forces. So,
whether it was the extraneous seeds of Confucianism, Buddhism, or, later
on, Catholicism, the resulting flowers were hybrids of native beliefs whose
roots were much deeper in the Vietnamese soil.

3

VIỆT NAM'S INDEPENDENT DYNASTIES

Neil Jamieson, a prominent historian of Việt Nam, claims that "Not until the Ly dynasty (1009–1225) did the development of what we now think of as traditional Vietnam begin to take shape."[1] To put that another way, the cultural seeds planted in Việt Nam during the first millennium CE sprouted after Việt Nam separated from China. This chapter is an exploration of Việt Nam's transition from a Chinese province to an independent state. Political freedom helped to establish native social patterns that continue to reflect Vietnamese enduring values.

THE LÝ AND TRẦN DYNASTIES

Chinese officials desperately tried to preserve China's glorious Tang dynasty (618–907) during its final years, but they were unsuccessful. The Tang decline provided Vietnamese leaders an opportunity to break China's thousand-year political rule over their land. In 938 a large Chinese naval fleet sailed into the Bạch Đằng River hoping that military force would prevent Việt Nam from seeking full-fledged independence. In a brilliant tactical move, however, the Vietnamese stuck bamboo stakes into the river's floor; the stakes' tips were just below the water's surface at high tide. Luring the Chinese ships up the river at high tide, the Vietnamese then waited for the tide to go out, leaving the Chinese vessels helplessly stuck in the maze of bamboo poles. The vast majority of China's ships were destroyed by the defending native forces. For the Vietnamese the Bạch Đằng victory marks the beginning of their country's independence.

For the remainder of the tenth century, Việt Nam struggled to find its footing as an independent state. Initially, the self-proclaimed Vietnamese king, Ngô Quyền (897–944), the architect of Việt Nam's Bạch Đằng victory, used the Chinese political paradigm to rule and proclaimed Cổ Loa as Việt Nam's capital city. These first steps of political autonomy

Figure 3.1. Boats on the Red River delta. Since the very beginning of Việt Nam's history, the delta has been an important source of water for farming and transportation. (Courtesy of Hoàng Việt, http://commons.wikimedia.org/wiki/File:Chua_Huong_059.jpg.)

were important but not long-lasting. As soon as Ngô Quyền died, China's continued threats made it clear that only a new political/social system would guarantee Việt Nam's sustained independence. So, rather than relying solely on the king's personal virtue to keep China at arm's length, a more pragmatic strategy was adopted, namely, Việt Nam's court nobility supported a large indigenous army and an impressive defensible capital to keep the country safe.

To accomplish these transitions, the Vietnamese incorporated both Chinese and Southeast Asian systems of political thought to establish a resilient state. Although the Vietnamese appreciated, and implemented, Confucian learning among the elite, like other Southeast Asians, they followed leaders whose legitimacy centered on a forceful personality. Thus, a king's prowess extended beyond military victories to the shaping of nature itself through communion with the unseen powers animating the universe: the ruler was ideally a spiritual superman.[2] With the support of the Buddhist Sangha (community), one such man, Lý Công Uẩn (974–1028), was made the paramount leader of Việt Nam in 1009, and the subsequent Lý dynasty lasted until 1225. The Lý emperors wore dragon tattoos and named their capital Thăng Long (Rising Dragon)—modern-day Hà Nội. Lý Việt Nam practiced a form of agrarian-based cult worship that helped define the rise of Thăng Long and the Lý family. The dragon symbol, along with altars for the gods of weather and grain, demonstrated the persistent influence of Việt Nam's earliest stories.

The first Lý kings used Việt Nam's military power to invade the lands of their southern neighbors, the Chams. Plundering their wealthy neighbors enriched the Lý kings and kept the taxes on Vietnamese farmers reasonably low. The Lý court was served by members of the Trần clan, and eventually the Trần took over the throne. The subsequent Trần dynasty (1225–1400) also used Thăng Long as its capital. The Trần kings feared that their advisers might follow the previous pattern in the Lý court and gain enough power to threaten the throne, so they took brides exclusively from within the Trần extended family. The Trần had also witnessed succession controversies in the Lý dynasty and their subsequent debilitating effects on the imperial system. To avoid such political debacles, Trần kings retired early and ruled behind the scenes while young monarchs grew into their imperial roles.

The Trần kings built on the Lý dynasty's domestic stability, but they faced unprecedented foreign crises, which resulted in both outstanding

Figure 3.2. The Hà Nội Citadel, which dates back to the Lý dynasty of the eleventh century. (Courtesy of Gryffindor http://commons.wikimedia.org/wiki/File:Panorama_of_Hà Nội .jpg.)

victories and catastrophic defeats. Apart from the regular Chinese incursions into Trần Việt Nam, an additional threat from a new global power came in the thirteenth century. Mongol armies threatened Việt Nam several times in the 1200s, and in each instance Vietnamese forces outlasted the invaders. Although the Vietnamese once again used bamboo poles to trap their enemy's boats in the Bạch Đằng River, the Mongols, fierce nomadic warriors from the region north of China, eventually occupied Thăng Long. The Mongols learned a lesson the Chinese already knew, and the French and Americans would learn many centuries later: occupying Việt Nam does not guarantee victory. The Mongols could not provide sufficient supplies to their army in Việt Nam, and the Vietnamese refused to cooperate with them. Thus Việt Nam was never incorporated into the massive Mongol empire.[3]

Champa, a neighboring kingdom located on the central coastal plains of modern Việt Nam, assisted Việt Nam in its wars against the Mongols. However, after the Mongols' 1287 withdrawal, Việt Nam began to decline while Champa's power increased. Quality of imperial rule, or the lack thereof, accounted for the respective rise and demise of both states. Professor Keith Taylor notes, "In the generations following the Mongol wars, the Trần clan gradually lost its taste for leadership."[4] Then, during the fourteenth century, Trần kings began taking secondary wives outside the Trần clan—a practice that had brought down the previous dynasty. As the Trần clan weakened, its in-laws exerted inordinate influence at the court until they eventually established their own short-lived dynasty. At the same time, the Cham royal leadership was particularly effective and Cham armies pillaged the weak and chaotic Vietnamese state. In 1371 Cham soldiers overran Thăng Long, plundering the capital right in front of the hapless Vietnamese imperial officials. The Vietnamese elite, desperate for relief from poor domestic leadership and Cham incursions, turned to China's vibrant Ming emperor for aid. For a second time, Việt Nam was incorporated into the Chinese system, but this time political subordination to China would last only two decades rather than a thousand years.

VIETNAMESE CULTURE

For more than four hundred years the Vietnamese enjoyed independence from China under the Lý and Trần dynasties. Political self-rule provided the stability needed to solidify the social mores that permeated Vietnamese culture. Việt Nam's writing system, a unique spiritual and philosophical worldview, and norms within family relations reflect three aspects of its cultural formation.

Written Vietnamese

The Vietnamese spoken language is related to the Mon-Khmer arm of the Austro-Asiatic linguistic group. However, an indigenous written script did not fully develop until the fourteenth century CE. Previously government officials and the literati had used classical Chinese characters for written communication, but in the 1300s the Vietnamese innovatively created a written language by developing their own characters. They first used Chinese characters to represent the sound of Vietnamese words, along with various tones. Designated Chữ Nôm, this script created new opportunities for aspiring poets and other writers, triggering a profusion of Vietnamese literature. This continued until Chữ Nôm was officially replaced in the early twentieth century by Quốc Ngữ, an alphabet-based Vietnamese script created by Alexandre de Rhodes (1591–1660), a French Jesuit missionary who came to Việt Nam in the seventeenth century.[5] Between the fourteenth and twentieth centuries, cultural battles over the use of Chữ Nôm versus classical Chinese (which candidates used for civil service exams) often ended with temporary bans against the use of either the foreign or the indigenous written script.

Religion

If a person were to ask whether the Vietnamese are Buddhist, Daoist, Confucian, or animist, an appropriate answer would be Yes! Once the Vietnamese gained political independence, they were able to freely practice native metaphysical rites and rituals; these customs were derived from a spiritual recipe that included ingredients from various faiths.[6] Most villages included an altar dedicated to the gods of agrarian enterprises, a Buddhist temple where monks provided educational opportunities for the community's children, and altars dedicated to ancestors in each home. And all the while daily life swayed to the rhythms of a harmonious Dao (Way) through

Figure 3.3. The French Catholic priest Alexandre de Rhodes, who romanized Vietnamese script in the seventeenth century. (In the US public domain.)

23

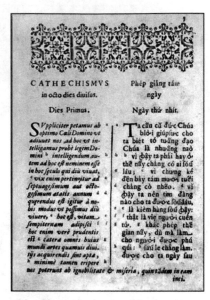

Figure 3.4. Quốc Ngữ translation of a Latin, Catholic catechism. Quốc Ngữ is romanized Vietnamese script. (In the US public domain.)

which one sought a proper balance in all things—hot/cold, male/female, sweet/sour, bright/dark. Westerners—almost all of whom grew up in traditions in which faith in one religion precluded adherence to another belief system—usually found it difficult to comprehend how the Vietnamese comfortably embraced a worldview that was a mixture of seemingly contradictory faiths. But the Vietnamese shaped these various ideas to fit their understanding and experience, and as changes occurred in their society they might adhere to one belief system more than another at given points in time. During the Lý and Trần dynasties, as would be the case in future Vietnamese dynasties, there were periods during which the Buddhist, Confucian, and folk religions waxed and waned, but no faith was ever extinguished thanks to the synchronistic nature of the Vietnamese metaphysical worldview.

Family

We know through myth and literature that during the Lý and Trần dynasties values related to family relations became more fixed as societal norms, and, ideally, the family became a microcosm of the state. For example, just as the emperor was the realm's absolute authority, the father absolutely ruled the home, and all under his roof dutifully deferred to him. Children learned that they had incurred a great debt to their parents for the gift of life and parental care. Even if sons or daughters rose to great wealth and professional prominence, their debt to those that gave them life actually increased because success was only possible by means of the life given to them. Within the home, male children enjoyed preferential treatment, including opportunities for education; younger brothers assumed a socially prescribed subordinate role to their elder brothers. Marriages focused on bringing two families together rather than two individuals. Thus they were based on arrangements between families rather than romantic love. To spare the embarrassment of a family's nuptial request rejection, village intermediaries (usually older women) acted as matchmaking conduits behind the scenes. Wedding ceremonies were simple: the groom made his way to pick up his bride in her home. Following his entrance into his in-laws' home and obligatory respect paid to their ancestors' altar, he would bring his bride to his home where she, too, paid respect to her new family's ancestors. Việt Nam was a patriarchal society, and a bride joined her husband's family, serving her husband and mother-in-law; she was also expected to bear sons.

While the social patterns established during the first native dynasties might appear neat and tidy, these descriptions were the ideal scenario and may not have always aligned with daily realities. Nonetheless, conventional patterns arose for everything from language to worship to family relations during the Lý and Trần dynasties.

CONCLUSION

Việt Nam's cultural roots certainly predate its independence from Chi-

Figure 3.5. Trần Hưng Đạo, the celebrated Vietnamese military commander who successfully fought off Mongol invasions during the thirteenth century. (Courtesy of Dennis Jarvis, http://commons. wikimedia.org/wiki/File:Statue_of_ Tran_Hung_Dao,_Ho_Chi_Minh_ City,_Vietnam.jpg.)

na. Yet it was during its earliest independent dynasties that a clear social demarcation helped to distinguish Việt Nam from China. However, as will be addressed in the next chapter, internal divisions weakened the Vietnamese ability to stave off serious external threats.

4

Internal Divisions and Westerners Arrive in Việt Nam

Several factors contributed to China's quick exit from Việt Nam after just two decades of rule (1407–1428). Due to Ming China's (1368–1644) expanding empire, its most effective officials had to govern its more significant geographical and political stations. Peripheral areas, including Việt Nam, were stuck with lower-level Ming bureaucrats. Vietnamese records report that the Ming representatives in the newly incorporated province of Đại Việt (Việt Nam) were scoundrels. In particular, Đại Việt–based Chinese bureaucrats and soldiers were motivated by economic profits rather than social improvements. Disgruntled Vietnamese gathered around Lê Lợi (1385–1433), the youngest son of a wealthy Vietnamese aristocratic family. Lê Lợi opposed Ming officials and their Vietnamese collaborators due to the overt exploitive nature of Chinese rule in Đại Việt. In 1428 Lê Lợi and his ragtag army defeated the Chinese forces in Việt Nam. Following his victory, Lê Lợi gathered the defeated Chinese soldiers along with Đại Việt Ming bureaucrats and ordered that they be safely escorted back to China. He wanted the Ming emperor to know that, although Việt Nam respected China's greatness, the Vietnamese desired to provide tribute as an admiring, independent state rather than a Ming province. Fortunately for Việt Nam, the newly enthroned Ming emperor, Xuande (r. 1425–35), had his hands full with internal and external troubles. These crises included continued Mongol raids on Chinese territory, the growing influence of eunuchs in the imperial system, and the decision to end China's massive fleet voyages around the waters of South and Southeast Asia.[1] China accepted Việt Nam's role as a tributary state. There would be future Chinese invasions, even as late as 1979, but Chinese leaders would never again attempt to make Việt Nam part of China.

THE LÊ DYNASTY

Following his 1428 military victory, Lê Lợi established himself at Thăng Long as Việt Nam's paramount political figure. The subsequent Lê dynasty (1428–1780) solidified Việt Nam as the region's dominant power. It was also Việt Nam's longest-lasting dynasty.

While some of the later Lê emperors ruled as puppets of powerful clans, the fourth emperor, Lê Thánh Tông (r. 1460–97), represented the height of the dynasty's imperial strength. Ascending the throne at nineteen years of age, Lê Thánh Tông appreciated the importance of information; he commissioned a detailed census for tax purposes. He also supported projects to maximize land for farming and financed hydraulic innovations that regulated water supplies for rice paddies.

Following the Chinese political model, Lê Thánh Tông used census data to divide Việt Nam into thirteen provinces governed by court-appointed officials. Passing the civil service exam, based on Confucian literature, remained the gateway into the Lê bureaucracy. But even more important than these logistical policies, Lê officials drew up 721 articles titled the Hong Duc Code; these regulations prescribed state penal and judicial laws. The Hong Duc Code is praised for its relatively favorable treatment of women—allowing them to own property and divorce irresponsible husbands; such ideas were anathema in China during that period, as women there were considered greatly inferior to men.

Việt Nam's domestic stability and prosperity under Lê Thánh Tông were developments that in part led to Vietnamese military incursions into Champa, a kingdom bordering southern Việt Nam. Vietnamese soldiers established military stations in the south, and in 1471 the Champa empire collapsed in the wake of Vietnamese invasions. Vietnamese landless farmers and entrepreneurs enjoyed unprecedented opportunities in the new southern provinces. Chinese merchants also found a more welcoming social culture in these new frontier lands where there was much greater ethnic diversity than in northern Việt Nam.

Powerful aristocratic and military families slowly encroached on Lê authority during the sixteenth century. One such family, the Mạc, actually forced the Lê emperor to flee into China, and between 1527 and 1592 the Mạc clan attempted to establish its own dynasty. However, the Lê emperors still had the nominal support of two powerful clans—the Trịnh and Nguyễn. So while Lê imperial rule reasserted itself over the Mạc, between 1600 and 1770 Trịnh and Nguyễn princes ruled behind the scenes.

Geography facilitated alliances between the Trịnh and Nguyễn. After some military battles and continuous jockeying for political position, the two families agreed that the Trịnh would control Việt Nam north of the Gianh River while the Nguyễn, with their capital at Huế, would exercise authority in the south; both families relied on the Lê emperors for legitimacy. The Trịnh named their portion of Việt Nam Đàng Ngoài or Tonkin; Dang Trong, or Cochinchina, were names for the southern, Nguyễn-dominated region.

Chaos, ineffective governance, civil strife, and outright rebellion characterized all of Việt Nam throughout the eighteenth century. In the north the aristocrats' greed resulted in numerous peasant uprisings. Traditionally, villages—not individuals—paid the state-required annual taxes. Farmers worked on "village" rice fields, assuming the communal nature of landownership and maintenance. Trouble resulted, though, when affluent families, some related to the Trịnh, challenged the village communal status quo by claiming communal lands as their own and requiring farmers to serve them as tenants. This upset the economic balance of Tonkin. Rice from village paddies had financed the imperial system for centuries. As communal lands were turned into private estates of the increasingly rich landholding class, the Lê court, weakened by Trịnh dominance, received considerably less revenue.

Trịnh advisers attempted to make up the ever-increasing revenue shortfalls by increasing taxes on the dwindling communal lands. They also placed new taxes on items such as salt and charcoal, resulting in an overwhelming strain on petty merchants, whose marginal profits evaporated because of these new state tariffs. In addition, severe famines in the 1730s and 1740s turned northern Việt Nam into a wasteland. Court records describe some hardest-hit areas as villages lined with the dead.

In the midst of such economic and social upheaval, many Vietnamese peasants simply abandoned their villages in search of a better life. Within a single generation the imperial court lost its historic tax base. Some of these wandering peasants joined revolutionary figures who claimed supernatural powers and preached apocalyptic messages. Nguyễn court documents at the time were also written in apocalyptic language. For example, one document notes that in 1775 "there appeared frequent strange signs: the earth moved, the mountains crumbled, the stars fell, the water turned red, the people suffered famine and bandits were everywhere. Throughout the land were seen these many spontaneous occurrences."[2]

Meanwhile, southern Việt Nam did not fare much better in the eighteenth century. The main problem for the Nguyễn was that Trương Phúc Loan, an adviser to the Nguyễn ruler, gained inordinate power and influence. Loan reportedly manipulated the legitimate succession order of the Nguyễn monarchs so he could dominate the weaker princes. In his position as regent to these young rulers, Loan raised taxes and accumulated great personal wealth. Furthermore, the Nguyễn economy ran out of copper, which was the basis of coinage in Việt Nam; they were forced to mint zinc coins, insisting that these now be used in the buying and selling of goods. Farmers did not accept this new coinage system and chose to hoard their rice rather than exchange it for inferior money. Less rice in the marketplace made its value increase, and peasants struggled under the weight of the Nguyễn's failed economic policies.

THE TÂY SƠN AND NGUYỄN DYNASTIES

Within these broken Vietnamese worlds, three siblings emerged. Known as the Tây Sơn brothers, they would end the Lê dynasty and prepare the path for Việt Nam's final dynasty. These future revolutionaries began their lives in a small village in Binh Dinh province. The eldest brother, a merchant of betel nut and an official tax collector, somehow got on the wrong side of Nguyễn officials. Fleeing for his life to the highlands, his two brothers joined him. They began preaching the message "Take from the wealthy, and give to the poor."

It might be best to designate Việt Nam's period between 1771 and 1802 as the Tây Sơn Wars because numerous victories and defeats occurred on all sides during these years. At the outset of their rebellion against the Nguyễn officials, the brothers claimed to possess superhuman powers and recruited highlanders who, against their normal isolationist preferences, supported the rebellion. Between 1771 and 1786 the Tây Sơn rebels allied themselves with the northern Trịnh/Lê armies to displace the Nguyễn ruling family. The brothers focused on Gia Định province, and Sài Gòn in particular, while the Trịnh/Lê pushed the Nguyễn out of the central plains and the city of Huế. One persistent

Figure 4.1. The French priest Pigneau de Behaine, who supported Prince Anh's successful military and political campaigns, which united Việt Nam. (US public domain.)

prince, Nguyễn Phúc Anh, would not give up! Despite multiple defeats, Prince Anh continued to lead his loyal troops and Siamese mercenaries against the Tây Sơn brothers. Finally, after humiliating losses, Anh retreated to the swamps and eventually fled to Phu Quoc, an island in the Gulf of Siam. There he found a patron in a French Catholic priest, Pigneau de Behaine (1744–98).

Figure 4.2. Gia Long, founder of Việt Nam's last dynasty, the Nguyễn (1802–1945). (US public domain.)

The eldest of nineteen children, Pigneau grew up in poverty in northern France as his father eked out a living as a tanner. Against his father's wishes, Pigenau entered the priesthood and rose in the clergy to become the bishop of Adran in India. The Frenchman, however, found fulfillment as a leader of the Catholic seminary in Phu Quoc, training Asian men for the priesthood. So when Prince Anh sought refuge at the island's seminary, Pigneau bet France's future in Việt Nam on the defeated but undeterred Nguyễn leader. Pigneau, along with Prince Anh's five-year-old son, Prince Canh, sailed to India and then France, pleading Anh's case. Despite other, higher priorities, King Louis XVI was persuaded to write a letter in support of Anh to French officials stationed in India's east coast city of Pondicherry. However, the king's dispatch was halfhearted, even including clandestine orders that the Pondicherry-based officials should disregard the letter's contents at their discretion. When Pigneau landed at Pondicherry on his way back to Việt Nam and discovered that, like the royal coffers, the king's promise was empty, he took it upon himself to organize a mercenary force of ships and troops to aid Prince Anh.

While Pigneau sought support for Prince Anh in India and France, the Tây Sơn rebels turned their attention north, successfully rooted out the Trịnh/Lê faction, and even defeated a substantial Chinese force of two hundred thousand troops sent to enthrone the legitimate Lê emperor. After this defeat the Qing emperor recognized Việt Nam's new dynasty, which the youngest Tây Sơn brother, who gave himself the name Emperor Quang Trung, established in 1787. This short-lived dynasty blossomed with many positive economic and social changes designed to relieve the burdens on Vietnamese farmers. Unfortunately, Quang Trung died just five years after

Figure 4.3. The Mieu Temple in Huế's Imperial City. Gia Long
and subsequent Nguyễn emperors made the central city of Huế
the imperial capital. (Courtesy of Trever Mills, http://commons.
wikimedia.org/wiki/File:The_Courtyard_-_The_Mieu_Temple.jpg.)

his imperial coronation, and at the same time Prince Anh was taking the
offensive in the south. The Tây Sơn followers could not recover from
the untimely death of their emperor and the southern attacks of Prince
Anh, who now had nominal support from the French through the work of
Pigenau. Prince Anh's army methodically made its way north until 1802
when the Tây Sơn loyalists surrendered Thăng Long to Nguyễn forces.
Prince Anh established the Nguyễn dynasty (1802–1945) and took the
imperial name Gia Long ("Gia" from Gia Định [Sài Gòn] and "Long"
from Thăng Long [Hà Nội]).

From all perspectives the Tây Sơn rebellion was a turning point for
Việt Nam. Surprisingly, Southeast Asian historians such as Bruce Lockhart
argue that the Tây Sơn rebellion's greatest contribution to Việt Nam may
have been losing: "The most significant long-term impact of the Tây Sơn
rebellion arguably lay in its defeat, since it paved the way for the Nguyễn
to take power, ruling over a stretch of territory larger than anything their
ancestors controlled."[3] Perhaps the brothers' most lasting legacy was that
future Vietnamese revolutionaries would refer to the Tây Sơn rebellion
as a precursor of twentieth-century Marxist-inspired movements. For just
as the Tây Sơn brothers guaranteed the poor Vietnamese that they would
end exploitation by the rich, the twentieth-century Vietnamese communist
leaders promised the same thing to their economically poor compatriots.

5

FRENCH IMPERIALISM IN VIỆT NAM AND NATIONALIST RESPONSES

I n 1802, Emperor Gia Long established Việt Nam's last dynasty, the Nguyễn (1802–1945). He knew from the outset that Việt Nam was broken and divided. Even though his military victories were just short of miraculous given the odds against him, these accomplishments proved easy compared to healing a partitioned country. During the 1700s Việt Nam was splintered and ruled by various powerful clans without the presence of a strong imperial system. War was the norm for the Vietnamese, and division characterized the political and social landscape. Given this context, Gia Long believed that Việt Nam would only thrive through benevolent, authoritarian leadership rooted in Confucian ideology. Using Qing China (1644–1912) as a model, the Nguyễn court mandated Chinese as the official language within the bureaucracy. The Nguyễn ministers wanted the state's social programs to adequately meet people's needs, but there was a high price to pay for a unified Việt Nam. Along with the implementation of a strict, authoritarian, Confucian ideology, Gia Long imposed draconian tax laws throughout the realm and reversed laws that treated women fairly. Huế, a centrally located city, became the Nguyễn imperial capital.

Gia Long's strict rule was not motivated by a malevolent spirit; rather, he firmly believed in following the pattern of Chinese emperors, who served as mediators between heaven and earth. Like ancient, sagacious Chinese emperors, Gia Long assumed that his careful, benevolent, and conscientious rule would ensure heaven's favor. He led important ceremonial rites and rituals promoting ancestor worship, Confucianism, agrarian deities, and heaven. Ubiquitous Confucian altars and temples evidenced the prominence of this ideology in Nguyễn Việt Nam. In 1807 Gia Long reinstated Confucian-based civil service exams, which were suspended during the eighteenth-century civil wars. Men who passed the tests managed the day-to-day affairs of state. From state to family levels, Vietnamese learned to follow a path of virtue as defined in the Confucian canon.

As Việt Nam intensified its commitment to archaic Chinese moral and political systems, the West raced toward modernity. While Việt Nam sought answers in ancient Confucian literature, the West placed its hopes in science, progress, and the future. Steam-powered engines ushered in a new world for Western nations, now competing against each other in a race for raw materials and markets to support their expanding economies and empires.

The English writer Herbert Spencer's theory of social Darwinism was another important catalyst for nineteenth-century Western imperialism. Based on Spencer's writings, Westerners assumed a cultural superiority over Africans and Asians, who were stuck in prescientific societies. Thus, as Rudyard Kipling famously wrote, it was the white man's burden to uplift non-Western peoples into the age of progress.[1] Consequently, of the eleven Southeast Asian countries, all but Thailand (then called Siam) fell under the rule of Western powers.[2] France imposed colonial rule over Việt Nam, which led to a difficult and sorrow-filled century for the Nguyễn emperors and their subjects.

FRANCE IN VIỆT NAM

France was a late arrival in the West's Southeast Asian colonial game. By the mid-1500s Portugal and Spain dominated portions of Southeast Asia, particularly with regard to interregional and international trade. By the late 1600s British, Dutch, and French traders had joined Portuguese merchants in Việt Nam, each group hoping to establish a viable economic enterprise. French priests were particularly pleased that the Vietnamese were receptive to Christian doctrines. Spanish friars had experienced even greater evangelistic success in the Philippines. But in contrast to the mostly pagan Filipinos, Vietnamese had deep ties to the Buddhist faith. Nonetheless, a great number of Vietnamese converted to Catholicism. The Vietnamese motives for conversion included the message of forgiveness of sins for every Christian believer, no matter what one's economic or social standing is. This was a message of equality that played well to the vast majority of Vietnamese who were not part of the economic elite or literati.

Gia Long enjoyed amicable relations with the French, particularly with Father Pigneau, who appeared in the previous chapter. Still, the first Nguyễn emperor's commitment to the Confucian worldview led

Figure 5.1. Rice fields in northeastern Việt Nam. Despite French rule, the daily routine of working in the fields continued throughout most of the country. (Courtesy of Doron, http://commons.wikimedia.org/wiki/File:TamCoc.jpg.)

him to choose a successor who embodied the xenophobic traits of the Chinese Qing emperors. Thus, Minh Mạng (r. 1820–41), Gia Long's son by a concubine, succeeded his father. Taking cues from his father and tutors, Minh Mạng ascended the throne with an anti-Christian agenda. In 1825 he instituted laws that forbade the practice of Christianity in Việt Nam. This did not diminish Việt Nam's growing economy. In fact the Vietnamese state did not consider economic interactions with the West particularly important since foreign trade continued through the Chinese merchant community. The second Nguyễn emperor continued the pattern of authoritarian Confucian rule. His dictatorial rule, along with staunchly anti-Christian laws, was ill-timed. One historian notes, "A more disastrous policy for preparing to cope with change in the external environment can scarcely be imagined."[3]

France's post-Napoleonic religious revival, French merchants' belief that the Mekong River in Việt Nam led to a navigable waterway into China, and the French navy's keen interest in the water passages of Southeast Asia led to civilian and military confrontations between France and Việt Nam. The fourth Nguyễn emperor, Tự Đức (r. 1847–83), was unpopular among his subjects. Although he tried to stand up to the French, ultimately

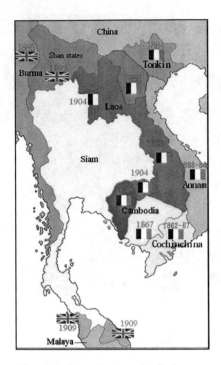

Map 5.1. French control of what became known as Indochina. The takeover was a gradual process. (Courtesy of Wikimedia Commons Atlas of the World, http://commons. wikimedia.org/wiki/File:French_ Indochina_expansion.jpg.)

the emperor presided over the transition from a unified, independent Việt Nam to a divided state controlled by the French. His policies were shortsighted, but there were few available options in dealing with the West.

When he ascended the throne, Tự Đức was determined to remove Christian influence among the Vietnamese once and for all. He ordered his officials to kill local and foreign priests. Catholic Vietnamese were branded on the cheek with the characters *ta dao* (infidel). France needed little further provocation to insert itself into Vietnamese politics. Tự Đức's policies and their consequences led to a French attack and occupation of Đà Nẵng in 1858; a subsequent, much larger French force of seventy ships and thirty-five hundred troops fought in the south and captured Gia Định in 1861.

Tự Đức's hapless response to the French attacks led to the 1862 Treaty of Sài Gòn. Provisions of the treaty included a large indemnity payment to France, the declaration of religious freedom for all Vietnamese, and French ownership of Gia Định and its three surrounding provinces. In the emperor's mind, these sparsely populated, ethnically diverse southern provinces were largely irrelevant to his rule, but he underestimated the implications of compromising with Western governments. In 1873 he was forced to cede the remaining southern portion of Việt Nam, identified as Cochinchina, to the expanding French empire. Nine years later the northern (Tonkin) and central (Annam) areas of Việt Nam became protectorates of France. The emperor and his court became mere symbols of the state as French colonial officials controlled Việt Nam.

In 1887, France organized its political influence in Southeast Asia by creating the Indochinese Union (ICU). This institution included Cambodia,

Tonkin, and Annam as protectorates and Cochinchina as a colony. Six years later Laos became France's fourth protectorate within the ICU.

VIETNAMESE INDEPENDENCE MOVEMENTS

Some observers might find it surprising that the Vietnamese did not initially offer more resistance to French control of their land. There were several reasons for Việt Nam's muted response to French encroachment. The main cause of Vietnamese indifference was the unpopularity of the Nguyễn emperors; harsh laws and increased taxes alienated the Huế-based Nguyễn bureaucracy from Vietnamese peasants. Bloody peasant protests fueled by famines, along with an occupying foreign power, convinced many Vietnamese that whatever heavenly blessing the Nguyễn regime might have had was long gone. Many Vietnamese intellectuals believed that society would improve under French rule but soon found that they had jumped from the wok into the fire.

France ruled Việt Nam with a heavy hand. French officials brutally suppressed any hint of independence movements. Over five thousand French officials oversaw Việt Nam's affairs. There were about the same number of British officials in India, *which was ten times more populous than Việt Nam.* French citizens established businesses and companies throughout Việt Nam. Known as French *colons*, these foreigners dominated Việt Nam's economy. For example, 90 percent of the rubber plantations—an important source of revenue—were owned by French. Furthermore, despite France's claim that its ultimate mission in Việt Nam was to bring civilization, French officials forcibly closed many schools. Literacy actually declined during the first decades of French rule.

Even so, Vietnamese viewed French rule with a mixture of admiration and irritation. As in other states in Asia and Africa, European imperialism brought with it awe-inspiring technology, which transformed mil-

Figure 5.2. Hồ Chí Minh. Hồ was one of many leaders who sought to eliminate foreign dominance in Việt Nam. (US public domain.)

lennia-old modes of transportation, energy extraction, health care, and agricultural life. A number of changes, particularly in transportation and public health, made life better for ordinary Vietnamese. For many European officials, however, colonies represented a blank canvas on which modernity could—and should—be painted. Governor General Paul Doumer, who ran Việt Nam from 1897 to 1902, was a quintessential example of the ambitious foreigner determined to imprint modernity on nonwhite peoples. Doumer's dizzying array of construction projects included road, railway, and bridge systems that modernized Việt Nam's transportation infrastructure. The Vietnamese were impressed with automobiles, trains, and other machines that were products of industrialization, although there was a steep price for foreign rule—someone had to pay for all the French officials, engineers, and industrialized machines. Doumer financed his endeavors by implementing crippling taxes on rank-and-file Vietnamese. The colonial government also established commodity monopolies and charged taxes on salt, opium, and alcohol. Taxes became so all-encompassing that the Vietnamese joked that deposits in the toilet were also subject to French taxes.

French rule in Việt Nam grew in intensity, as did Vietnamese resistance. Generally speaking, the reaction to French rule can be chronologically and thematically described as immediate outrage, paths that differed from traditional Confucian protests, and nationalism paved with Marxist ideology.

Immediate Outrage

By 1884 all of Việt Nam was subject to French rule. France placed a young emperor, Hàm Nghi (1872–1943) on the throne that same year, hoping imperial counselors would fall in line behind its chosen ruler. But Nghi and his regent, Tôn Thất Thuyết (1839–1913), had other plans. In the summer of 1885, the emperor and Thuyết fled to the mountains, calling on all their subjects to defend the sovereign and expel the French. The movement was spurred by an edict titled Con Vuong, or "Loyalty to the King." France simply replaced Hàm Nghi and pursued the renegade emperor and his advisers. Three years of gallant but ultimately futile fighting in the name of Hàm Nghi ended when the French captured the former emperor and exiled him to Algeria.

New Ways

The failure of active and bloody resistance to French rule clearly signaled that the old system was forever gone. Nguyễn intellectuals concluded that there were three options for dealing with the strange new world they faced. First, many chose to withdraw from public life and service. These intellectuals believed that the tsunami of French dominance could not be stopped and resistance was futile. They would neither support nor resist French rule.

A second group of scholars was not as ready to capitulate to foreign rule. Led by Phan Bội Châu (1867–1940), these men promoted terrorist acts to restore an independent Nguyễn prince. This literati faction was particularly inspired by Japan and China. During the first part of 1905, Phan traveled to Japan seeking support for the restoration of a strong imperial system. He was pleasantly awed by Japan. By the winter of 1905, Japan was the only non-Western industrialized state, having successfully begun this phase of economic development between 1875 and 1900. In May 1905 Japan's Imperial Navy crushed Russia's Baltic Fleet at the Battle of Tsushima, a victory that spelled the end of the Russo-Japanese War. Furthermore, Japan's copper mines and textile factories, among other industries, made it an emerging global economic force at the turn of the twentieth century. Phan rushed back to Việt Nam, picked up a prince he hoped would lead his country to freedom, and returned to Japan. A movement led by Phan and other like-minded Vietnamese called Travel East encouraged Vietnamese students to study in Japan and learn from their Asian neighbor. Part of Phan's plan to restore an independent emperor included terrorist attacks against French colonial officials. Indeed, various French officials were murdered in Việt Nam during the first decade of the twentieth century; in 1912 an assassination attempt was even made against Governor General Sarraut.

Other Vietnamese scholars chose a third way. This group believed that the answer was neither silent retreat nor a fight with the French; rather, Việt Nam's best option was to collaborate with the French, learn from foreigners, and cooperate in modernizing Việt Nam until the Vietnamese could stand on their own. Many in this group found encouragement in China's 1911 Revolution, which did away with the imperial system. In the Tonkin region these pro-French scholars used the growing popularity and accessibility of Quốc Ngữ (romanized Vietnamese script) to publish journals that encouraged Vietnamese to admire French civilization and cooperate with the existing government. Since all Quốc Ngữ publications required French approval, it is not surprising that these Tonkin-based journals praised French rule.

Things were different in Cochinchina, where the southern Vietnamese were directly ruled by the French. Large tracts of land in the Mekong delta were sold to wealthy Vietnamese families, which dominated Cochinchina's social scene. The local affluent families had to walk a political tightrope: since the French colonial government was responsible for their prestigious economic and social positions, these families might suffer losses if a grassroots, anti-French, movement gained traction. But, as members of the Vietnamese elite acquired excellent French-based educations, they sought greater representation in the Colonial Council, Cochinchina's legislative body, which was dominated by French bureaucrats. When the French refused to increase Vietnamese representation on the council, the landed elite turned its attention to ousting competing Chinese merchants and entrepreneurs from Vietnamese society.

In the end, none of the approaches by Vietnamese scholars and aristocrats diminished French control of Việt Nam during the first decades of the twentieth century. It was time for a new approach with new ideas.

Marxism and Nationalism as Answers

A new generation of Vietnamese nationalists burst onto the scene in the mid-1920s, including Hồ Chí Minh, whose life and work made him the most recognized Vietnamese person in the twentieth century. Hồ was born in May 1890 and raised in Nghệ An province—a region well known for fighting foreign rule. His father, a teacher who refused to use the French language in the classroom, wandered the country as an itinerant tutor. Nonetheless, he sent his son to a local French-language school, believing that to defeat an enemy one must first learn from it.

When he was about twenty, Hồ moved south and served as a village schoolteacher. Finding himself in Sài Gòn in 1911, he signed on as a crew member on a French ship and began a new type of education—training based on global travel, extensive reading, and human interaction. Between 1911 and 1917, Hồ spent time in the Middle East, the United States, and England working at odd jobs and honing his linguistic proficiency in English, Russian, and Cantonese, as he spent time in New York's Chinatown.

Throughout the world of nineteenth-century Western imperialism, colonial subjects who sought to either collaborate with or fight against their colonial masters often studied in their masters' homelands: Filipinos moved to Spain, Indonesians to Holland, Indians to England, and Vietnamese to France. More than a hundred thousand Vietnamese traveled to France during World War I and assisted the Allies' war effort. Paris became Hồ's ultimate destination in his globe-trekking adventures, and he settled there in 1917, working to help thousands of his countrymen navigate the strange sights and sounds of Europe at war.

While in Paris Hồ was attracted to the politics of the socialists and their emphasis on social justice and human rights. For men like Hồ, World War I represented an opportunity to throw off the yoke of colonial rule. British diplomats promised Arab officials that they would support their independence from the Istanbul-based Ottoman Empire. President Woodrow Wilson of the United States also advocated greater self-determination for colonies, which was in line with the socialist doctrine Hồ admired.

At the close of the war, the Paris Peace Conference of 1919 proved to be a great disappointment for the Vietnamese nationalists, who had hoped for some discussion of independence for Asian colonies. As William Duiker, the definitive biographer of Hồ Chí Minh, noted about the Paris Peace Conference, "Frustrated demands for national independence [at the conference] drove countless patriotic intellectuals from colonial countries in Asia and Africa into radical politics."[4] Hồ was both disappointed and disillusioned by the conference's outcome, but he found solace in his growing attraction to Vladimir Lenin's "Thesis on the National and Colonial Questions." Lenin's thoughts convinced Hồ that socialism alone would not free Việt Nam from French domination. Consequently, he became a founding member of the French Communist Party, moved to Moscow, and developed political ties with Russia's Communist leaders. In 1924 Hồ moved to Canton in southern China; the following year he helped found the Đoàn Thanh niên Cộng sản (Communist Youth League). This organization, led by Vietnamese students trained by Hồ, began to grow in Việt Nam. Small groups coalesced around the ideology of Marxism, and the writings of Hồ, a man who had left Việt Nam fifteen years earlier on a French freighter, were becoming popular.

In December 1927, two years after Hồ helped found the Communist Youth League, another Vietnamese nationalist organization came into existence. The Việt Nam Quốc Dân Đảng (Vietnamese Nationalist Party or VNQDD) was founded through the efforts of Hà Nội–based teachers dedicated to the teachings of Dr. Sun Yat-sen and the Chinese Nationalist Party (Kuomintang or KMT). Between 1925 and 1927, northern Vietnamese KMT followers translated and published literature that promoted indigenous nationalist movements. To increase Vietnamese literacy, teachers offered classes on Quốc Ngữ.

To its credit, the VNQDD worked with other nationalist Vietnamese organizations. But it faced three daunting hurdles it could not clear. First, financial problems plagued the organization from the outset. The VNQDD's leaders decided to open a hotel and restaurant (the Việt Nam

Hotel) where they could have secret meetings while also using the facilities to earn money for the movement. Even with financial support from the KMT and the Việt Nam Hotel, the VNQDD lacked the economic resources to advance its message. Money problems also contributed to the movement's second difficulty: faulty communication systems between the various VNQDD units. This was particularly disastrous when the VNQDD tried to instigate a general uprising against the French in a February 1930 revolt. The VNQDD's third challenge was that it was several years behind Hồ's organization—a movement that indoctrinated both the peasants and urban workers in Marxism's anti-imperialist worldview. These difficulties for the nationalist party were exacerbated by increased French vigilance against any independence movements in the late 1920s. Spies within the VNQDD made it rather easy for the French to suppress the nationalist uprising, sending hundreds of its members to prison and executing its leaders when the revolt failed.

The Communist Youth League competed with other, newly formed Vietnamese communist organizations, and at times these groups were at odds with each other. After the successful 1917 Bolshevik Revolution, Russia directed communist movements around the world through the Communist International (Comintern) organization founded in Moscow in 1919. Since Russian leaders knew Hồ Chí Minh, they asked him to merge the various Vietnamese Communist parties into a single entity.

Following the Comintern's orders, Vietnamese communist leaders met in Hong Kong on February 3, 1930, with Hồ presiding. These multiple groups became one entity, the Indochinese Communist Party (ICP). The primary initial goal of the ICP was to drive the French from Indochina. Various grassroots ICP associations were organized and legitimized at a 1930 Hong Kong conference.

The excitement, anticipation, and optimism that followed the founding of the ICP was quickly dashed by brutal setbacks. First, in 1931 Hồ Chí Minh was arrested in Hong Kong by British agents; fortunately, some of Hồ's influential friends protected him from extradition to Việt Nam, which most likely saved his life. In Việt Nam the global economic depression had caused Vietnamese rice farmers, rubber plantation workers, and urban employees to sink to unprecedented levels of poverty. In the midst of the economic crisis, French troops descended on Nghệ An province to mercilessly destroy any trace of communist activities. Airplanes dropped bombs on suspected communist communities, and thousands of rank-and-file communists, along with most of the ICP leaders, were rounded up and imprisoned. It was not an auspicious beginning for the Communist Party in Việt Nam.

Hồ's imprisonment in Hong Kong lasted less than two years. On his release he moved to Moscow, where he spent the next six years studying and teaching at various institutions, including the Lenin Institute. Meanwhile, massive global geopolitical changes were about to displace French rule in Việt Nam. On July 7, 1937, Japanese troops stationed in the newly created state of Manchukuo (Manchuria) invaded China. Two years later Germany invaded Poland, plunging Europe into World War II.

In 1940 Japan and Germany signed an alliance treaty, France fell to Hitler's troops, and Japanese soldiers occupied northern Việt Nam. A year later, in July 1941, the Japanese moved into southern Việt Nam with the permission of France's pro-German Vichy government. It was a time of chaos—a perfect opportunity for the beleaguered Vietnamese communists to regroup. The communists also provided economic and political stability for thousands of Vietnamese caught in the surreal world of Japanese occupying troops, nervous French collaborating officials, and formerly prestigious Chinese Vietnamese families now losing everything to the Japanese.

Communist leaders joined Hồ Chí Minh in February 1941 near the Việt Nam–China border and spent their time formulating a strategy to liberate Việt Nam. Hồ and his colleagues had to be especially careful because Japan's occupation had brought with it a renewed anti-communist policy due to its alliance with the vehemently anti-Marxist Nazi Germany and Japan's vicious battles with Mao Zedong's Chinese communists. While occupying Việt Nam, Japanese soldiers removed all vestiges of communism from the urban areas. This only reinforced Hồ's thesis that an effective revolution had to begin with the common people—the rural farmers.

In February 1941 all of these concerns were discussed and important resolutions were passed. For example, ideological stridency was to take a backseat to a more inclusive fight for national independence. A new group was formed that enlisted all who shared the goal of independence; it was called Việt Nam Độc Lập Đồng Minh Hộ (League for the Independence of Việt Nam) or Việt Minh for short. This revolutionary organization took solid hold in Việt Nam's northern Viet Bac area and slowly spread south so that Hà Nội eventually became an urban island of imperialism in a sea of anticolonial rural villages.

The French-Japanese alliance broke down in March 1945, and French officials and soldiers were imprisoned. Japan declared an independent Việt Nam headed by Emperor Bảo Đại, a scion of the Nguyễn family. At the same time, a severe famine, the result of both bad weather and Japanese policies, cost at least half a million Vietnamese lives between March and May 1945. Pragmatic Vietnamese communist leaders fighting the Japanese found rather unusual allies in the United States and French citizens toward the end of the war. Thanks in part to these coalitions, the communists provided food for the starving peasants, which engendered goodwill toward the Việt Minh.

CONCLUSION

In one of history's greatest understatements, Japan's Emperor Hirohito noted in an August 15, 1945, radio broadcast that the war "did not turn in Japan's favor, and trends of the world were not advantageous to us. . . . [T]he war situation has developed not necessarily to Japan's advantage."[5] In fact, from the time of Japan's defeat at Midway in June 1942, the Japanese struggled to maintain their bloated empire.

Following Hirohito's speech, the Việt Minh wasted no time. On August 28 it established a temporary government under the title the Democratic Republic of Việt Nam (DRV). Emperor Bảo Đại resigned, and imperial rule in Việt Nam came to a final end after almost two thousand years. A few days later, on September 2, 1945, in front of a million Vietnamese, Hồ Chí Minh climbed a stage in Hà Nội and declared the independence of Việt Nam. He began his speech by partially quoting Thomas Jefferson's words from the US Declaration of Independence: "All men are created equal. They are endowed by their creator with certain unalienable rights; among these are life, liberty, and the pursuit of happiness." At the end of his talk he noted, "Việt Nam has the right to enjoy freedom and independence and in fact has become a free and independent country. The entire Vietnamese people are determined to mobilize all their physical and mental strength, to sacrifice their lives and property in order to safeguard their freedom and independence."[6] For millions of Vietnamese, their lifelong dream of freedom appeared to have reached a successful conclusion with the majestic words of Hồ on that warm September day. *It was not to be.*

6

THE TWO VIỆT NAM WARS

It is hard to picture a darker world than the one the Vietnamese faced following Hồ Chí Minh's September 2, 1945, declaration of independence speech. Internally the Vietnamese were facing massive starvation in the north. In southern Việt Nam millions of Vietnamese joined the new religions of Cao Đài and Hòa Hảo. These metaphysical movements attracted desperate and disenfranchised Vietnamese searching for meaning in an absurd world of war and chaos.

NEW RELIGIONS

Founded shortly after World War I, Cao Đài blended Buddhist, animist, Daoist, and Christian teachings, particularly emphasizing ethical behavior and benevolence toward all creatures. It attracted Vietnamese who were disgusted with a world gone amok, providing consolation in a faith that promised eternal rewards for a life emptied of selfishness and filled with compassion. In 1939 a Vietnamese mystic began preaching a Buddhist-based religious system, which called for people to internalize their Buddhist faith. The emphasis in this new sect, known as Hòa Hảo, was personal devotion to an inner spiritual life as opposed to participation in numerous temple-based rituals. Both Cao Đài and Hòa Hảo incorporated apocalyptic elements in their doctrines, and many disheartened Vietnamese converted to these faiths, which promised an impending metaphysical rescue. Enthusiastic nationalists alongside starving farmers and heaven-gazing spiritualists characterized a less than united Việt Nam. This social context led to political chaos.

While the northern DRV army moved south, Japanese units provided little resistance to the Việt Minh. But to their dismay, Việt Minh units met increased resistance as they approached Sài Gòn.

In a prearranged agreement among the Allies, the British and Nationalist Chinese accepted the Japanese surrender in southern and

Figure 6.1. A worshiper offers incense in the Quan Am Pagoda in Hồ Chí Minh City. The new Vietnamese religions of Hòa Hảo and Cao Đài combined elements of indigenous beliefs and world religions. (Courtesy of Franzfoto, http://commons.wikimedia.org/wiki/File:Ho_Chi_Minh_City_-_Quan_ Am_Pagode_17.jpg.)

northern Việt Nam, respectively. Two hundred thousand poor, hungry, and fortune-seeking KMT troops occupied northern Việt Nam while the British in Sài Gòn released French colonial officials and helped reinstate French control in Cochinchina.

A 1946 agreement between the competing parties resulted in the KMT withdrawal, the French recognizing the DRV within the French Union, and the DRV acknowledging that southern Việt Nam remained under French authority. Despite this arrangement, however, the Việt Minh were determined to eventually liberate all of Việt Nam. Meanwhile many French colonials still behaved as if they were above the law in northern Việt Nam. Within the DRV, Vietnamese port officials insisted that French merchants submit to inspections; angry exchanges gave way to hostilities, with French ships bombarding the northern coastal city of Hải Phòng in late November 1946. An eight-year war ensued.

THE FIRST VIỆT NAM WAR, 1946–1954

As at the beginning of a sporting event, most people are supportive and enthusiastic at the outset of a war. France saw an opportunity for national redemption in Việt Nam following its military difficulties during World

War II. The Việt Minh hoped this war would expel the French and unite an independent Việt Nam. But it was not a quick war, lasting longer than World War II. While the French enjoyed naval and air superiority, the Việt Minh used the vast countryside to hide in after hit-and-run operations. French soldiers were relatively safe within Việt Nam's cities, but in the rural areas—which made up most of the landscape—the Việt Minh courted peasant support, making it dangerous for the French to venture away from urban places. Clashes between Việt Minh and French soldiers took a devastating human and economic toll on both sides. In France the initial support for maintaining a colony in Southeast Asia faded as the mounting casualties and atrocities perpetrated by both sides were made public. The French press began to refer to the conflict as *la sale guerre*, "the dirty war."

Võ Nguyên Giáp was the primary strategist for the Việt Minh. A well-educated lawyer and former history teacher, Giáp insisted that Vietnamese peasants learn to read so they could learn communist doctrines of anti-imperialism. Earlier in his life, Giáp had suffered a great loss when French officials imprisoned his wife and daughter; both died while incarcerated.

In 1954 Giáp directed Việt Minh soldiers to help the communist Pathet Lao in neighboring Laos. These troop movements in northwestern Việt Nam exposed large numbers of Việt Minh. The French general Henri Navarre concluded that a conventional battle between the French and Việt Minh might be possible on the Việt Nam–Laos border. Furthermore, the French were determined to stop Việt Nam's communists from linking up with their Laotian ideological comrades. Navarre decided to take a stand in the valley village of Điện Biên Phủ, located between the mountains that bordered Laos and Việt Nam. More than fifteen thousand French troops dug in at Điện Biên Phủ during the spring of 1954. Điện Biên Phủ, the conventional battle Navarre longed for after years of fighting guerrilla warfare, ended in the worst disaster for the French in the annals of modern colonial warfare. The French mistakenly assumed that their superior air power would tip the battle in their favor; however, thick foliage, inclement weather, and heavy fog helped conceal the Việt Minh in the mountains surrounding Điện Biên Phủ. Giáp's soldiers also painstakingly carried large cannons up the mountains. Once in place and effectively concealed in the foliage, these large guns pounded the helpless French army. On May 7, 1954, more than eleven thousand French soldiers surrendered to the Việt Minh—the largest surrender of a colonial army in modern history. In an auspicious coincidence, May 1954 also marked the beginning of negotiations between the French and Việt Minh in Geneva, Switzerland.

Numerous diplomats gathered in Geneva during May 1954 to seek a solution to the eight-year war in Việt Nam. America sent its top diplomats, including Secretary of State John Foster Dulles; the Chinese sent their foreign minister, Zhou Enlai. Việt Nam had become a major issue in the Cold War—a pawn in a chess game that neither side was willing to sacrifice. In fact, by 1954, the United States was financing 80 percent of the French war effort in Việt Nam. Yet the United States was disheartened. Mao Zedong had defeated the pro-American Chinese Nationalists in 1949; the North Koreans, along with the Chinese Communists, had fought the United States to a stalemate in the 1951–53 Korean War; and now France was looking for a way out of its mess in Việt Nam.

After weeks of tough negotiations in Geneva, an agreement between the French and Việt Minh was brokered largely through the diplomatic efforts of Zhou Enlai. France agreed to withdraw from Việt Nam provided that the Việt Minh and their DRV government would only control territory north of the seventeenth parallel. South of this line, France's ally, the former emperor Bảo Đại, and his prime minister, Ngô Đình Diệm, would lead the anticommunist Republic of Việt Nam (RVN). A plebiscite scheduled for 1956 would allow the southern Vietnamese to choose whether to unite

Figure 6.2. Different parties in Geneva try to come to an agreement to end the first Việt Nam War. (US public domain.)

with Hồ's DRV or remain a separate state. So, like East and West Berlin and North and South Korea, Việt Nam fell victim to the divisions of the Cold War. But neither the Việt Minh nor their counterparts in South Việt Nam were pleased with the Geneva agreement. In fact the leaders of South Việt Nam and their ally, the United States, refused to sign the treaty. For their part, the Việt Minh leaders felt unduly pressured by the Chinese into accepting a divided Việt Nam despite their victory at Điện Biên Phủ.

Figure 6.3. Ngô Đình Diệm greeted by US President Dwight Eisenhower. Diệm received American support as the leader of the Republic of Việt Nam. (US public domain.)

Following the 1954 settlement, more than one million northern Vietnamese abandoned their homes and moved south; these were mainly Catholics, business owners, members of the upper classes, and others who believed in private markets or had special ties to the French. The refugees feared that a harsh Marxist-based ideology and economy would threaten their lifestyles or beliefs. This was a wise move on their part as the DRV leaders quickly abolished the rich landholding class and nationalized major portions of the economy.

In southern Việt Nam the French withdrawal created an economic and political vacuum that the United States filled. Based on its own intelligence reports, the United States chose to support Diệm in the RVN 1955 national elections. Diệm was a single, devout Catholic who had spent time in New York and New Jersey seminaries and also had lived in a Belgium Benedictine monastery. Fully devoted to his homeland, Diệm believed he knew what was best for Việt Nam. Along with his Catholic convictions, Diệm had a deep-seated commitment to Confucian philosophy, particularly in regard to familial loyalty and the unquestioned authority of rulers. Winning the 1955 election over his rival Bảo Đại by a somewhat unbelievable 98 percent, Diệm set out to establish a free and prosperous South Việt Nam after almost a century of French rule, two world wars, and a costly eight-year war with France.

But Diệm faced crises that he could not solve. In short he had to contend with the northern communists who sent spies into the south to spread Marxists beliefs and advocate for a united Việt Nam under Hồ Chí Minh. Faced with this outside interference, Diệm refused to hold a Geneva-directed plebiscite in 1956. Furthermore, given the weakness of the Army of the Republic of Việt Nam (ARVN), Diệm had to rely on US military advisers and aid to prop up his government and army. But the more US support the RVN received the more vulnerable Diệm was to the communists' accusation that South Việt Nam was still a semicolonial state. Diệm was trapped: if he refused US aid, his regime would collapse; if he accepted US economic and military support, he would be accused of being America's puppet.

Việt Nam between the Wars

Following the 1954 division of Việt Nam at Geneva, southern Vietnamese farmers, a group that made up 90 percent of the RVN population, were caught in the middle of a global battle to win their hearts and minds. Việt Minh cadres infiltrated South Vietnamese villages, speaking against Diệm and his US advisers, while the RVN attempted to improve the economic and social lives of its citizens. South Vietnamese communists, with help from the DRV, established the National Liberation Front (NLF), a clandestine organization that offered a Marxist-based political system as an alternative to the RVN.

South Vietnamese farmers enthusiastically accepted support from RVN officials. The Japanese and French departure from their economic and social worlds signaled a return to the life of rice planting along with the seasonal rhythms of rites, festivals, and religious ceremonies. But the routine of farm life did not last long. Continued harassment by Việt Minh and ARVN soldiers once again placed the poor farmers in the middle of competing armies. Diệm tried to keep the rural population safe from Việt Minh propagandists by building walls around villages and, at times, even moving entire villages into newly constructed safe compounds; but what was meant for good turned out to be disastrous. Farmers, whose lives heretofore were rarely regulated, even when the French and Japanese controlled the area, were now told where they had to live.

What the RVN considered a safe place for farmers was viewed by the South Vietnamese communities as well-regulated concentration camps. American funding also facilitated a dramatic increase in the number of ARVN soldiers and consequently greater interference in the usually calm countryside. Diệm's regime grew unpopular among the South Vietnamese, even to some within the political system. Rather than aligning themselves with the Việt Minh, many South Vietnamese RVN detractors tried to bring about change without violence. Yet Diệm and his American supporters considered anyone who opposed RVN policies a traitor and collaborator with the northern communists. The South Vietnamese RVN detractors were labeled as Việt cộng even though some of them initially had little or no affiliation with the Việt Minh or NLF.

South Vietnamese did not find peace under the Diệm regime. They also resented his nepotism toward family members. Diệm's older brother, Ngô Đình Thục, was the Catholic archbishop of Huế while his younger brother, Ngô Đình Nhu, controlled the ARVN. Growing criticism of the Diệm regime was met with brutal suppression and punishment by ARVN soldiers, who took their orders from Nhu. At the same time, American military advisers bitterly complained about the ARVN's reticence to fight the real enemy—the communists. Diệm's limited support among the Vietnamese virtually ended when his government attacked a Buddhist parade during a festival in Huế in May 1963; during the breakup of the festival, one woman and eight children died. It was not lost on the Vietnamese that the authoritarian ruler of the predominantly Buddhist RVN was a devout Catholic. This persecution of Buddhists was turned into an effective propaganda tool against the Diệm regime.

To protest the abuses against Buddhists, Thích Quảng Đức, a sixty-six-year-old Buddhist monk, sat in a busy Sài Gòn street intersection on June 11, 1963. After being doused with gasoline, Đức lit a match and burned to death as reporters and onlookers watched in reverence, awe, and horror. Rather than responding with compassion, Diệm's family ridiculed the monk's sacrifice; Madame Nhu, wife of Ngô Đình Nhu, trivialized the self-immolation as nothing more than a barbecue.

South Việt Nam was coming apart. Top ARVN officers began a plot to overthrow Diệm and Nhu, even approaching US officials to see if the United States would support a coup. American diplomats were likewise unhappy with Diệm and the social mess he had helped create. In one of his last interviews, American president John F. Kennedy indicated that Diệm had to make changes if he wanted further US support. He noted:

> In the final analysis, it's their (Vietnamese's) war. They're the ones who have to win it or lose it. We can help them, we can give them equipment, we can send our men out there as advisers but they have to win it—the people of Vietnam against the Communists. We're prepared to continue to assist them, but I don't think that the war can be won unless the people support the effort, and in my opinion, in

the last two months the government has gotten out of touch with the people. . . . With changes in policy and, perhaps, within personnel, I think it [the RVN government] can [gain the support of the people]. If it doesn't make those changes, I would think that the chances of winning it would not be very good.[1]

Diệm was trapped in his Confucian political philosophy, and he was not about to change. On the morning of November 2, 1963, Diệm and Nhu were taken prisoner in an internal military coup and promptly murdered. Their mangled bodies were placed in the back of a truck and photographed—a grisly reminder of what can happen to those who rely on America's support and have that support withdrawn.

North Việt Nam did not experience the political turmoil that plagued its southern neighbor between 1954 and 1963. Hồ's popularity and the absolute power of the Vietnamese Communist Party (VCP) helped DRV officials implement land reforms that eliminated the wealthy landholding class. From 1954 to 1957 North Vietnamese farmers enjoyed the new system in which they worked their own land while paying moderate taxes; this was a far cry from the previous pattern of slaving away for absentee landlords at subsistence wages. But prosperity did not come to the vast majority of the North Vietnamese between 1958 and 1963. Economic disaster in China between 1958 and 1961 meant that China could not provide its normal assistance to Việt Nam. This led DRV officials to demand that Vietnamese farmers pool their resources and provide more grain for the Hà Nội–based government. More than thirty thousand cooperatives, each one encompassing approximately eighty-five families, essentially stripped DRV farmers of their lands; labor and harvests were now exclusively for the state. America's increased presence and support of South Việt Nam meant that all DRV citizens had to make sacrifices in order to remove Western imperialism from Vietnamese soil.

Much was changing behind the DRV's political curtain. There was an internal battle between those convinced that the DRV should concentrate on domestic issues and those who believed the government's priority should be reunification. Led by Lê Duẩn, the faction advocating North-South reunification triumphed over its political rivals. In 1960 Lê Duẩn was elected secretary of the VCP, and he remained in that post until his death in 1986. Throughout the 1960s, as Hồ's health deteriorated, Lê Duẩn took the reins of power, masterfully playing China and the Soviet Union against each other as both countries continued to heavily support the DRV.

THE VIỆT NAM WAR

Removing the Diệm regime only increased the political and social chaos in South Việt Nam as one coup followed another. The only constant was a steady—turning into a raging—stream of US economic and military support for the fledgling RVN government.

America's determination to prop up an anticommunist, free market, prodemocracy regime in the RVN was matched by the DRV's resolve to eliminate the US presence in Việt Nam and unite the country under the banner of a communist, state-controlled economic system. As the stakes of the global Cold War increased, so, too, did the overt US presence in Việt Nam. Confrontation and conflict were inevitable. The shot heard around the world signaling DRV and US hostilities took place a few miles off the coast of northern Việt Nam in the Gulf of Tonkin. During the first week of August 1964, US destroyer ships claimed they had been fired on by the DRV, prompting the US Congress to pass the Tonkin Gulf Resolution. This piece of legislation authorized the US president to use whatever means necessary to protect South Việt Nam. The resolution passed unanimously

Figure 6.4. Sky Crane CH-54A helicopter used by the United States during the Việt Nam War. Despite superior technology and weapons, the United States could not defeat the Vietnamese communists. (US public domain.)

in the House of Representatives while only two senators cast dissenting votes. Like France two decades earlier, America was initially supportive of a war in Việt Nam.

Following the passage of the Tonkin Gulf Resolution, US planes began bombing strategic targets in North Việt Nam. Many wondered whether the DRV—a newly created, small Southeast Asian state—stood a chance against the world's greatest superpower. But North Vietnamese officials saw this war as a contest for the soul of their beloved homeland. Some Americans, particularly journalists, warned the United States that the Việt Nam conflict represented potential humiliation and defeat for America. As early as 1965, David Halberstam brilliantly laid out this doomsday scenario in *The Making of a Quagmire: America and Vietnam during the Kennedy Era.*

American troops were sent to fight in Việt Nam. By 1968 more than 500,000 US soldiers were on the ground in South Việt Nam. By contrast, at the height of US troop presence during the Iraq and Afghanistan wars, there were 166,300 and 101,000 US soldiers, respectively, in those foreign lands.

Insisting that the RVN adhere to democratic principles in the midst of the chaos, South Việt Nam held elections in 1967 with the darling of the military, Nguyễn Văn Thiệu, winning a plurality of votes. Backed by the ARVN and America, President Thiệu continued the policy of belligerence against the Việt Minh and NLF. Like Diệm, Thiệu continually pleaded for more American aid, yet reports indicated that corrupt ARVN officials exaggerated the number of soldiers in their fighting units so as to receive additional American dollars. This ruse made the lying officers rich, but it crippled the undermanned ARVN forces in the field.

The war drove the economies of both North and South Việt Nam as both states depended on assistance from foreign governments. In North Việt Nam, this help consisted of military weapons, including modern fighter planes and antiaircraft guns. Việt Minh forces fighting Americans used unconventional tactics such as guerrilla warfare for which large weapons were superfluous. But for the RVN foreign aid included not only military equipment but also a large foreign presence. Almost three million American military personnel served in Việt Nam during the war. South Việt Nam's economy was not only directed toward the war effort, but it also became focused on servicing young American soldiers. Bars, prostitution, and an active black market transformed South Việt Nam's urban landscape as rural folk fled the danger of the war for the alluring promise of American dollars in the cities. The subsequent breakdown of traditional

Vietnamese social values added another reason for the war's unpopularity among many South Vietnamese.

Many experts on the Việt Nam War believe that the NLF's 1968 Tết Offensive was the war's turning point. Tết, the lunar New Year and Việt Nam's most celebrated holiday, ushered in 1968 with much more than firecrackers. Directed by North Vietnamese military officials and carried out mainly by the Việt cộng, the communists simultaneously attacked South Việt Nam's

Figure 6.5. Mass graveyard for communists who died trying to capture Huế during the 1968 Tết Offensive. For the Việt cộng, the battle was a military disaster but a political victory. (US public domain.)

urban centers on January 30. Việt cộng soldiers infiltrated the US embassy, and the Imperial City of Huế was held by the communists for several days. However, the grassroots uprising the NLF hoped would support its attacks did not materialize. In short the Tết Offensive was a military disaster for the Việt cộng, but politically it worked to perfection. Western media captured American officials ducking for cover in their pajamas outside the US embassy; cameras also captured the horrific scene of a South Vietnamese military official publicly executing a suspected communist sympathizer. These scenes caused many Americans to reassess US involvement in an increasingly unpopular war. Walter Cronkite, the highly respected CBS anchorman, broadcast an editorial predicting that the final outcome of the war would be more like a stalemate than the promised US military victory. Subsequently, President Lyndon Johnson did not run for reelection in 1968 and the Republican nominee, Richard Nixon, became the next US president. He promised an American victory in Việt Nam.

President Nixon, along with his security adviser, Henry Kissinger, tried to gain the upper hand in Việt Nam with a three-pronged approach. First, they rekindled talks with the DRV, hoping that diplomacy might provide a way out of the war. However, the North Vietnamese would only negotiate if the United States stopped bombing North Việt Nam. Meanwhile, US military officials insisted that the bombing was imperative for the RVN's safety. Second, President Nixon instituted what he termed "the Nixon Doctrine," also called the "Vietnamization" of the war. Nixon and his aides hoped the ARVN would take full responsibility for defending South Việt Nam rather than continuing to rely on US troops.

The third and most controversial Nixon-Kissinger strategy concerned Việt Nam's neighbor, Cambodia. Led by a popular king turned politician, Norodom Sihanouk, Cambodia prospered through the 1960s under Sihanouk's strategy of neutrality—a difficult foreign policy position during the Cold War. Within Cambodia there was a very small contingent of rural communists known as the Khmer Rouge. But throughout the 1960s they could not advance their Marxist agenda in Cambodia because economic prosperity characterized the country's rural and urban population. But while Sihanouk's leadership brought wealth to Cambodians, he did not have the power to change Cambodia's geography. American officials concluded that the Vietnamese communists were using sanctuaries in Cambodia to plan and launch attacks against the ARVN and US soldiers. So, without the approval of Sihanouk or the US Congress, President Nixon ordered a secret bombing campaign on the neutral territory of Cambodia. Sihanouk publicly denounced the bombings, claiming that the real victims of the US bombs were innocent Cambodian farming families. Sihanouk's supposed acquiescence to communist sanctuaries on the Việt Nam–Cambodia border upset US officials. Thus, the United States did nothing to stop a military coup against Sihanouk on March 17, 1970. The new Cambodian leader, General Lon Nol, and his generals overtly aligned themselves with the United States. The following month the new Cambodian government allowed US and RVN troops into its country to seek out and destroy all Vietnamese communist base areas on the Việt Nam–Cambodia border. American advisers, officials, weapons, and dollars began flowing into Cambodia, which President Nixon termed "the Nixon Doctrine in its purest form."

Nothing worked for Nixon in Việt Nam. No matter what the RVN and the United States tried to do, Vietnamese communist soldiers persisted in their military, political, and ideological fight for Việt Nam's reunification. In Cambodia the ousted Sihanouk sided with the Khmer Rouge through the intermediary efforts of China. Almost overnight the fledgling Cambodian communist community mushroomed into a dynamic, numerically impressive army that threatened the pro-US military government centered at Phnom Penh.

In Việt Nam the war continued with mounting casualties, including countless civilians caught in the crossfire. Thiệu continued to serve as the RVN's president following his 1971 reelection, while Lê Duẩn's DRV leadership grew even more prominent following the September 2, 1969 death of Hồ Chí Minh. With President Nixon's landslide reelection in 1972, it appeared that with the same leaders in place the war would simply continue. But large segments of the US population were now against the war, and there were calls for Nixon's impeachment when Congress learned about the secret Cambodian bombings. North Việt Nam was also somewhat concerned about China's level of genuine support following Nixon's 1972 visit there. Still, the DRV believed that it was negotiating from a position of strength as the various parties met between 1968 and 1973 to find a compromise that might lead to peace.

In the end, without fully consulting President Thiệu, the United States, DRV, RVN, and NLF signed the Paris Peace Accords on January 27, 1973. The agreement stipulated that a cease-fire would take place immediately and all the US troops and other foreign soldiers would withdraw within sixty days. For its part the DRV agreed to recognize the RVN and use democratic processes for possible future reunification. In exchange the DRV agreed to release US and ARVN prisoners. While President Thiệu complained about the terms of the treaty, he was privately given assurances that President Nixon would use air power should the DRV military invade South Việt Nam. However, the US president was soon embroiled in the Watergate scandal, which led to his resignation. American promises to support the RVN vanished as domestic, social, and economic turmoil engulfed the presidency of Gerald Ford. The DRV and RVN resumed hostilities in 1974, and the ARVN rapidly lost ground to its enemies. The Khmer Rouge was also overwhelming Lon Nol's troops in neighboring Cambodia. On October 17, 1975, the Khmer Rouge marched into Cambodia's capital, Phnom Penh, and ousted the pro-US regime. Thirteen days later Vietnamese communist troops eliminated the final remnants of the RVN in Sài Gòn. The wars were over, but new ones were around the corner.

7

POST-INDEPENDENCE TURMOIL

May 1, 1975, was the first twenty-four-hour period in more than 113 years during which Việt Nam was united. Foreign and civil wars were over for the Vietnamese. Before his death, Hồ Chí Minh predicted that Việt Nam would be "10,000 times more beautiful" following the country's reunification.[1] Unfortunately, the years following reunification were some of the hardest in Việt Nam's history. How could so many monstrous disasters follow such hard-won military and political victories? This chapter recounts the 1975–85 decade of sorrow for Việt Nam.

DISASTROUS POLICIES

"And, in practice, it [Lê Duẩn's post-1975 policies] all worked about as well as might be expected, which is to say not at all. Popular discontent grew, and by late 1979 the Vietnamese economy had ground to a near halt."[2] This insightful statement by Frederick Brown, a fellow at the Johns Hopkins Foreign Policy Institute, sums up the years immediately following Việt Nam's reunification. Certainly this did not match the great optimism of DRV leaders immediately following their April 30, 1975, final victory in Sài Gòn. Lê Duẩn, a top DRV leader, summed up the bright future he expected for Việt Nam: "Now nothing more can happen. The problems we have to face now are trifles compared to those of the past."[3] Lê Duẩn was so full of hope that he guaranteed that in a decade every Vietnamese family would own a radio, television, and refrigerator. Such optimism notwithstanding, Việt Nam was entering troubled times. Other nations' policies had negative effects on Việt Nam, but many of its postwar wounds were self-inflicted.

Following reunification, DRV leaders were divided over the country's policy priorities. Those who were more liberal cautioned against trying to force North Việt Nam's tightly state-controlled economic system on the southerners. In stark contrast, the hard-line Marxists, led by Lê Duẩn, insisted that the North's economic paradigm be immediately implemented in the South. At the 1976 Fourth Party Congress, the Lê Duẩn faction won out, and Việt Nam was given the new state title of the Socialist Republic of Việt Nam (SRV). The party projected that its policies would transform the SRV's economy so that within two decades Việt Nam would move beyond small-scale industry to a full-blown, large-scale, industrial economy. This was an unrealistic goal given the VCP's insistence on strict state control. Nevertheless, the government kept making promises—it began writing checks it couldn't cash! David Marr and Christine White, editors of an important book, *Postwar Vietnam: Dilemmas in Socialist Development,* note, "In short, at the end of the war, the leadership not only expected to work miracles; miracles were expected of it by the population."[4] Unfortunately, the SRV leaders had no miracles for the people.

Lê Duẩn and his advisers radically misunderstood what South Việt Nam needed in order to become a productive partner of the North. Examples from a 1975 statistical survey of Việt Nam starkly indicate the level of human and physical devastation:

- 20,000 bomb craters
- 362,000 war invalids
- 10 million refugees
- 1 million widows
- 880,000 orphans
- 250,000 drug addicts
- 300,000 prostitutes
- 3 million unemployed
- 5 million hectares of destroyed forests
- two-thirds of the nation's villages destroyed[5]

By 1975, 40 percent of South Việt Nam's population had fled from rural battlegrounds to the cities. In addition, two hundred thousand of South Việt Nam's professionals escaped with their American allies before Sài Gòn was overrun by communist troops. After so many years of war, what South Việt Nam needed was tender care; what it received instead were harsh, punitive actions by its northern former enemy. Once in control of the entire country, North Vietnamese officials sought out former ARVN officers and others who had collaborated with the Americans. More than a million southern Vietnamese were sent to reeducation camps to repent of their past ideological sins and learn the values of communism. A general rule was that high-ranking ARVN officers were to spend twelve years in reeducation while ARVN captains and majors were sentenced to eight years of political retraining. Rank-and-file ARVN soldiers only spent months or weeks in these camps.

To alleviate the pressure on South Việt Nam's cities, SRV officials set a goal of transplanting four million of its citizens into New Economic Zones (NEZs) between 1976 and 1980. These zones were semifrontier areas that were undeveloped due to their remoteness and lack of infrastructure. To populate these areas, young volunteers were sent to Việt Nam's more inaccessible territories where they constructed sustainable farms for the urbanites. Vietnamese families were promised newly built homes, seed, fertilizer supplies, and land if they would relocate. But the NEZs were not popular. Only about a quarter of the projected numbers accepted the government's offer because, among other things, many found the NEZs to be poorly planned—resembling concentration camps more than economic opportunities.

Making matters even worse in the South, SRV leaders seemed to ignore the fact that, in addition to substantial US aid, since 1954 South Việt Nam's economy had been linked to an international market system. Although it was not one of the world's wealthiest states, the RVN had made substantial economic gains because of its participation in a global free market system. Farmers in the RVN were relatively prosperous, though often harassed by the ARVN, Việt cộng, and Việt Minh. The SRV leaders' decision to abruptly dismantle and replace South Việt Nam's economic system created financial and social chaos. As the economy ground to a halt, officials realized that if people were to remain farmers they needed incentives rather than rhetoric and state-improvement goals. When the SRV eliminated entrepreneurial activities and privately funded enterprises, many South Vietnamese responded by trying to leave the country. Hundreds of thousands of South Vietnamese pursued illegal means to escape their country in hopes of holding onto their movable assets. These refugees became known as "boat people" because so many left Việt Nam in small vessels. These little boats were sometimes captured by pirates who abused passengers and stole their possessions. Thus, postwar South Việt Nam experienced both a brain drain (professionals leaving with the Americans) and an economic vacuum due to the exodus of the boat people.

THE SUBSIDY DECADE

Things were not much better in North Việt Nam. The 1975–85 decade in northern Việt Nam was so miserable that Vietnamese assigned the

Figure 7.1. The SRV banner flies atop Hà Nội's Flag Tower. (Courtesy of Chinasauer, http://commons. wikimedia.org/wiki/File:Flag_ tower,_Hà Nội .jpg.)

moniker *thời bao cấp* (subsidy period) to these ten years.[6] While the idea of a subsidy might sound helpful, for many this meant that the only hope for survival hung on the benevolence of surly state officials who exchanged rice and other goods for state-issued coupons. It was not unusual for people to stand in line for half a day to make such transactions. Guards had to monitor the queues as fights broke out when individuals argued about their place in line. There were also stories of local cadres distributing coupons based on bribes. This illegal reselling of state-issued coupons contributed to a prevailing atmosphere of pessimism and cynicism among urban North Vietnamese.

In North Việt Nam's rural areas, farmers questioned the SRV's demand that all grain had to be sold at state-determined prices to government-approved agents. It is probable that the SRV did not anticipate this increasing defiance by heretofore compliant farmers. However, after the war the situation changed for North Vietnamese farmers. During the conflict, DRV farmers were motivated to do their part in sacrificing for the state. Many farming families had a relative involved in the war; thus, resources were willingly provided at least in part because farmers were supporting a son, daughter, husband, or wife who was fighting for the motherland. Even before the war, farmers gave most of their harvests to the state, and in exchange for grain the government gave farmers commodities sent to the DRV from China. This encouraged farmers to work for the state in a quid pro quo arrangement of sorts. When American bombs were dropped on the DRV during the war, farmers were reminded that the very existence of their country hung in the balance. After the war ended, it made no sense to continue selling grain at ridiculously low state prices. The situation became even worse when imported commodities from China dried up because of a political crisis between the two states (see chapter 8 for more on this conflict).

Despite such economic and social upheaval, SRV leaders persisted in advancing their agenda of state control. They intended to show the world that the SRV was, according to Lê Duẩn, "an impregnable outpost of the socialist system, an important factor of . . . national independence, democracy, and social progress in Southeast Asia."[7] The DRV's rhetoric and insistence on a pure ideology could not feed the Vietnamese. With both the North and South Vietnamese economies reeling, the threat of starvation loomed. The anthropologist Ken MacLean writes that "during a decade [1975–85] in which inflation peaked at 775 percent, an estimated 70 percent of the population lived beneath the poverty line, and chronic food shortages meant fifteen million people nationwide were either severely malnourished or on the edge of starvation due to insufficient calories."[8]

While some southerners escaped this brutal decade through harrowing boat travel, thousands of northern Vietnamese found relief by working in the Soviet Union and other Soviet bloc countries. By 1982 fifty thousand Vietnamese were employed in the Soviet Union and other communist countries' factories. Conditions in these industrial plants were harsh; critics of the SRV published claims that Vietnamese labored in Siberia—working as virtual slaves. While Vietnamese officials denounced such criticism, the sad fact was that, according to the Institute of Southeast Asian Studies research officer Ng Shui Meng, "By whatever measure, the living standard even in the poorest socialist bloc country would compare favourably to that in Vietnam."[9] Stories of desperate Vietnamese bribing local cadres for just a chance to work in foreign industrial plants proliferated during the early 1980s. One bright spot regarding foreign work was that Vietnamese returned home with food and other resources to help alleviate local conditions.

LOOKING BACK: 1975–1985

Vietnamese are reluctant to speak at length about the decade following the war. For many those ten years represent a nightmare they wish to forget. Paradoxically, the subsidy years also served to bring out the best in the Vietnamese. While there was corruption among the cadres, most Vietnamese used the daily struggle for existence to draw closer to each other. Just as the Vietnamese had banded together to push out the Chinese, Mongols, French, Japanese, and Americans, they found solace in community during the postwar years. As one Vietnamese stated, "I recall [the subsidy period] as a time of hardships, but also greater equality in society."[10]

Another positive aspect that came out of this dark decade was the creation of new opportunities for ordinary Vietnamese. Scores of independent businesses emerged because of the hard times. To be sure, most of these economic opportunities were simply backyard shops; still, these endeavors were seeds for larger, overtly independent entrepreneurial activities in the 1990s and beyond. The subsidy era's makeshift businesses grew because no new items were coming into Việt Nam so anything that was broken needed to be repaired or repurposed. Consequently, bike repair experts, tailors, and other such craftsmen learned to push the limits of usability so that ragged clothes would be wearable and bike chains would continue to turn patched wheels down the streets of Việt Nam.

Some Relief

Việt Nam's economic desperation was so acute that by 1979, just three years into the life of the SRV, the party was forced to reassess its goals and plans. Hard-core Marxist politicians had much to answer for, and there was not much they could say. At the Sixth and Ninth Plenums of September and December 1979, the VCP approved a program of "output contracts."[11] In short the government would allow farmers to sell their surplus grain (above the state-determined quota) in open markets at prices that the market—not the state—determined. This economic concession to a partial open market did little in the short term to improve Việt Nam's economic and social conditions. It took almost two years for the output contracts to be implemented. The delay was partially due to the doctrinaire communists' continued resistance to moving away from complete state economic control. Then, once farmers were finally able to sell their surplus crops, the demand was so much greater than the supply that prices skyrocketed. As inflation approached 1000 percent annually, hard-line Marxist politicians tried to rein in a runaway economy by cracking down on the embryonic free market system. A horrendous cycle of ill-considered economic policies plunged Việt Nam even deeper into chaos. It was not until 1986 that a more moderate approach began to put Việt Nam's economy onto a more stable track.

Conclusion

Studying this decade of Vietnamese history is difficult due to the lack of available material. Fortunately, since Việt Nam opened up economically after 1986, more information has been forthcoming about its postwar years.

But why did all this misery have to happen? How could Lê Duẩn and his advisers get it so wrong after the monumental victory over South Việt Nam and its foreign allies? Several considerations might help us understand the thoughts of the postwar DRV officials. First, Lê Duẩn and his closest advisers were fully convinced that Marxism was the only ideology worth pursuing and that solutions to social and economic problems could only be found in Marxist-Leninist thought. Unbending in their conviction and dismissive of any idea that veered from their ideology, Lê Duẩn and his cadres plunged the SRV into orthodox Marxism believing this was the magic pill the entire country must swallow. They were wrong.

Fear on the part of postwar DRV leaders was another motive for implementing such a harsh system. They even mistrusted their communist comrades in the south, forcing them to disband the NLF. Thus, if the North Vietnamese communists feared their own southern ideological brothers, one can only imagine their fear of former American-supported RVN and army personnel. It was partially out of this fear that DRV officials came to believe that a harsh peace was required for a prosperous, unified Việt Nam. Again, they were mistaken.

Finally, victories can be dangerous. Mao, Napoleon, Hitler, and countless other leaders ruined their societies after great victories. Frederick Brown truly captures this tragic pride in postwar Việt Nam with these words: "And hubris, the sort of pride that comes naturally to people who have won a great victory, also played a role in determining Vietnam's self-destructive course—and not just at home but beyond its borders as well."[12] Intoxicated with success, DRV officials could hardly imagine that their postwar policies might not be right.

Unfortunately for Việt Nam, Lê Duẩn and his advisers failed in their postwar economic and social strategies. We will see in the following chapter how these blunders were compounded by a foreign policy that plunged Việt Nam once again into a decade-long war.

8

VIỆT NAM, CAMBODIA, AND THE WORLD, 1975–1989

A united Việt Nam entered a troubled world. In 1975 the Cold War still pitted communist countries against the United States and its allies. Even between communist states, however, there were significant clashes. China and the Soviet Union were moving in opposite directions with their domestic and foreign policies. The United States was recovering from President Nixon's resignation, the aftereffects of the Việt Nam War, and an oil crisis. These global situations compounded Việt Nam's domestic crises described in the previous chapter. It is hard to imagine a worse foreign relations scenario than the one Việt Nam faced between 1975 and 1986.

The end of the war completely changed Việt Nam's domestic and foreign circumstances and policies. During the war years (1954–75), the DRV received substantial support from the People's Republic of China (PRC) and the Soviet Union. South Việt Nam existed on the largess of the American economy. After the war ended, foreign aid ceased as well. After the death of Mao Zedong in 1976, China transitioned from a socialist economy to an era of more economic pragmatism. Even before the end of the war, relations between North Việt Nam and China were strained due to a thaw in US-China relations and the DRV's close relationship with China's rival, the Soviet Union. After the war, the United States was not about to support the newly united Socialist Republic of Việt Nam (SRV) and refused to accept its legitimacy. America reneged on its 1973 promise of a three-billion-dollar economic package to help rebuild Việt Nam and also pressured its allies to follow suit.

THE CAMBODIAN WAR

While these difficult foreign relations hampered Việt Nam's chances for postwar prosperity, it was its neighbor Cambodia that completely drained Việt Nam's resources until the 1990s. It is a sordid story but one that must be understood to help clarify Việt Nam's postwar struggles.

Earlier in this book we learned that the communists in Cambodia, known as the Khmer Rouge (Red Khmers), grew in power following America's bombing of Cambodia and the military coup against the popular President Sihanouk. Khmer Rouge leaders, including Saloth Sar (Pol Pot), Ieng Sary, and Khieu Samphan, embraced Mao Zedong's idea of relying on farmers' hard work to create a strong economy. Following the fall of Cambodia to the communists in April 1975, Khmer Rouge leaders began to unfold their hideous plans to cleanse their country of any perceived opposition. They emptied the capital, Phnom Penh, and placed the entire country's population in rural communes where all life was strictly regulated and executions were common.

While for millions in Cambodia this reign of terror resulted in loss of life, for the Khmer Rouge leaders, this was the beginning of a radically different way of life. They christened 1975 Year Zero and changed the country's name from Cambodia to Democratic Kampuchea (DK). These cosmetic changes did not mask unspeakable horrors committed by the Khmer Rouge and their minions. Torture, ethnic cleansing, and murders of tens of thousands defined the policies of DK officials. Because the Kampuchea-engineered utopia could not have religion, Christian, Buddhist, and Islamic leaders were eliminated. Even those who wore eyeglasses were suspected of being intellectuals and were persecuted and killed.

What disturbed Việt Nam the most were the Khmer Rouge policies toward Vietnamese living in Cambodia. Cambodian leaders not only wanted an agrarian utopia, they also wanted a "pure" society, which to them meant the elimination of any group tainted by foreign influence. When Cambodian communists who had lived and fought in Việt Nam returned home, the Khmer Rouge executed not only them but also their families! If the Khmer Rouge murdered their own ethnic communist brothers, they were even more brutal to Vietnamese living in Kampuchea. Vietnamese fortunate enough to escape from DK returned to Việt Nam with unbelievable tales of teenage Khmer Rouge soldiers roaming the land, seeking to torture and kill all Vietnamese residents.

From the outset, DK leaders encouraged their soldiers to cross into Việt Nam and exact revenge for past crimes committed against Cambodia; these crimes included the ARVN illegally entering Cambodia with the aid of American advisers during the early 1970s. Kampuchea, along with other Southeast Asian countries, believed that Việt Nam still intended to dominate the former Indochina area (Laos, Cambodia, and Việt Nam). Even though cross-border battles occurred in which entire villages were massacred, a semblance of politeness characterized official DK and SRV relations. Politicians visited each other and sent congratulatory messages on various victory anniversaries over past US-leaning regimes. But these diplomatic niceties disguised the hatred, overt military attacks, and sophisticated battle strategies for what many in both countries believed was a looming war.

The last thing that the embryonic SRV needed was another war, especially since its own economy and society lay in ruins. But the Khmer Rouge attacks were too brutal to ignore. Furthermore, Việt Nam did in fact see itself as the country with

Map 8.1. The Vietnamese-Cambodian border. The extent of this border is one reason why disputes have occurred between the two countries. (US public domain.)

the most authority among the former Indochina states. Vietnamese blood spilled at the historic battles of Điện Biên Phủ and Khe Sanh to stave off French and American imperialism legitimized Việt Nam's assumption that it was the bastion of a socialist society; regional deference was due for such sacrifices and victories. Therefore, SRV officials would not stand by as DK soldiers crossed into Việt Nam, slaughtering civilians and then returning to the safety of Cambodian soil. But there was something even larger at stake—China.

Relations between the PRC and the Soviet Union were never strong. Communist countries around the world often had to choose the patronage of one or the other. Fortunately for Việt Nam, both communist behemoths lent support while the DRV fought the Americans. But Việt Nam, sharing a border with its huge neighbor, had always been wary of China. In the past the Vietnamese had experienced Chinese invasions, occupations, and political assimilation. President Nixon's 1972 surprise visit to Beijing caused DRV officials to again question China's friendship, as it appeared that US-PRC relations might be warming at the expense of the DRV. Just as the Việt Minh were not properly supported by China at the 1954 Geneva conference, the PRC again seemed to betray its communist comrades south of its borders.

Then, in 1976, just as the SRV and DK were trying to smooth things over diplomatically, everything in China changed. With the death of

Mao and the subsequent arrest of his wife and other architects of China's Cultural Revolution, China began moving away from strict ideological orthodoxy to greater economic and social pragmatism while Việt Nam's policy makers moved in the opposite direction. China was also displeased that Việt Nam had fostered close ties with the Soviets. Chinese officials suspected that the Soviet Union was merely using Việt Nam to spread its influence in Asia. But China had its own ally in Southeast Asia: Democratic Kampuchea. The DK's leaders began heavily relying on China for resources and global legitimacy.

An ominous pattern began to emerge during 1977 and 1978 as both the Soviet Union and the PRC increased their supply of weapons to Việt Nam and Kampuchea, respectively. Emboldened by these newly acquired Chinese arms, the DK kept up its harassment of Vietnamese villagers, seemingly oblivious to Việt Nam's much larger population and military prowess.

By the summer of 1978, Vietnamese leaders concluded that the only solution to the continued DK harassment was an all-out battle to remove the Khmer Rouge from power. As Việt Nam's military responses against the DK in eastern Kampuchea became more severe, Pol Pot and his advisers began criticizing their own army for not winning battles against the Vietnamese forces. In fact DK leaders ordered that punitive attacks be carried out against their own Kampuchean army in the eastern zone! This internal turmoil, along with the three-year senseless massacre of the Cambodian people, compelled some eastern-zone DK commanders, including Heng Samrin and Hun Sen, to flee across the border and join the Vietnamese.

As more Khmer Rouge defectors trickled into Việt Nam with tales of a three-year genocide in their own country, Việt Nam organized them into a small army, supported by over sixty thousand Vietnamese soldiers, called the People's Volunteer Army (PVA). Despite a Chinese warning to the DK government of an impending invasion, the PVA crossed into Kampuchea on December 25, 1978. Within days it had eliminated one-half of the entire DK army. Cambodian civilians were too weak to oppose the Vietnamese, and most felt a sense of relief as the brutal Khmer Rouge cadres fled west toward the Thai border. But Việt Nam's intentions were not simply to punish the Khmer Rouge and temporarily displace it. Within three weeks the Vietnamese fully and completely uprooted the DK leadership and its political infrastructure! By mid-January 1979, the PVA had pushed the Khmer Rouge into Thailand where Red Cross stations cared for the displaced Cambodians. To legitimize and consolidate its victory, Việt Nam installed Heng Samrin as the new leader of a country that was now called the People's Republic of Kampuchea (PRK).

If Việt Nam expected that it would be thanked for destroying one of history's most brutal regimes, it was mistaken. International response to the invasion of Cambodia was generally one of outrage. Within the United Nations (UN), the United States and China took the lead in denouncing Việt Nam, and the UN decided to recognize only the Khmer Rouge's DK as Cambodia's legitimate government. Even Cambodia's former president and king, Norodom Sihanouk, asked the UN to recognize the DK rather than the Việt Nam–supported PRK. Economic sanctions against the PRK notwithstanding, the UN condemnation of Việt Nam was mostly rhetoric. However, China intended to give Việt Nam more than just a rhetorical scolding.

As the PVA swept the Khmer Rouge from Cambodia in early 1979, Mao Zedong's successor in China, Deng Xiaoping, kept his eye on the Southeast Asian war. On January 1, 1979, the United States officially recognized the PRC, and Deng responded with an official state visit. While in the United States, Deng told American officials that at times children must be punished. What Deng meant by this axiom was that China was about to discipline its prodigal son, Việt Nam. On February 17, 1979, more than two hundred thousand Chinese troops crossed into Việt Nam, engaging the Vietnamese army in heavy fighting. The Chinese overran several of Việt Nam's northern cities and threatened to march on Hà Nội. But, given the fighting experience it had gained in recent wars against the French, American, and Khmer Rouge militaries, the Vietnamese army did quite well in opposing the Chinese. China claimed it had accomplished its goal of teaching Việt Nam a short, swift lesson, and its army returned to the safe confines of Chinese territory. While the Sino–Việt Nam War lasted just a few weeks, it reportedly resulted in more than one hundred thousand deaths. The war also reminded both countries of their volatile relationship.

China's invasion did not change Việt Nam's commitment to its war in Cambodia. The reality was that the PVA could not withdraw because a number of Cambodian indigenous armies had clandestinely organized to try to regain control of their country. Even the murderous Khmer Rouge received military aid from both China and the United States to harass the PVA. The pitiful state of the Cambodian people constituted an even greater tragedy. If ever there was an entire nation that suffered from post-traumatic stress disorder, it was the PRK. In 1979 Cambodia was in ruins because of the devastating three-year rule of the Khmer Rouge. Orphans, widows, widowers, thousands of people missing limbs, and ubiquitous land mines dotted Cambodia's social and geographic landscape. Furthermore, there was very little on which to build a solid civilization. The Khmer Rouge had eliminated most of Cambodia's educated professional class. Both the UN and the United States blocked humanitarian aid for the Việt Nam–backed PRK, leaving it up to the Vietnamese to sustain and rebuild Cambodia. As was described in the previous chapter, Việt Nam could not even adequately provide for its own population, much less a neighboring state. Still, Việt Nam would not abandon the PRK. It stationed the PVA in Cambodia to fight recalcitrant Khmer Rouge guerrillas, as well as other foreign-supported Cambodian freedom fighters.

Throughout the early 1980s, Việt Nam sought a solution to its Cambodian quagmire. It invited Sihanouk to join in rebuilding the PRK and promoted open elections in 1985. When the former Khmer Rouge defector Hun Sen won the election and became the country's prime minister, the international community again accused Việt Nam of simply setting up a puppet state now governed by a pro-Vietnamese Cambodian official. China and the United States were particularly relentless in condemning Việt Nam for its continued Cambodian occupation.

Massive Soviet economic support undergirded Việt Nam's Cambodian occupation. Moscow probably paid Việt Nam to remain in Cambodia so that it would continue to be a thorn in China's side. But as each year passed in the 1980s, Soviet officials grew increasingly tired of supporting Việt Nam's war in Cambodia. Finally, when the Soviet Union collapsed in 1989, so did its economic support for the PVA.

CONCLUSION

After ten years of fighting for and supporting the PRK, the PVA was replaced by the United Nations Transitional Authority in Cambodia. Việt Nam's withdrawal from its neighboring country was more face saving than the 1975 US withdrawal from Sài Gòn; still, both countries learned a hard lesson about trying to occupy and prop up a friendly government in a foreign land.

Việt Nam's post-1975 years were difficult. Domestic policies were misguided and ineffective. Foreign relations, apart from the alliance with the crumbling Soviet Union, were colored by continued US anger at Việt Nam and the regime's seemingly unprovoked invasion and decade-long domination of Cambodia. But just as Mao's 1976 death signaled a change for the Chinese, Lê Duẩn's 1986 passing signaled a new and brighter day for the Vietnamese.

9

Modern Promises and Problems in Việt Nam

During the 1990s, Việt Nam became the planet's second-fastest-growing economy; that same year Hồ Chí Minh City (HCMC) became the fastest-growing urban economy in Asia. In a matter of just a few years, Việt Nam transitioned from widespread malnutrition and a need to import rice to being the world's third-largest rice exporter. Its gross domestic product (per capita) jumped from $114.00 in 1992 to $1,191.00 in 2010, and its poverty rate shrunk from 58 percent in 1993 to 10 percent in 2010 (lower than the US poverty rate of 16 percent). If you have read the last three chapters, these statistics might make you scratch your head. An even more remarkable aspect of Việt Nam's 1990s economic prosperity is that during this time its political system barely changed. Yet not all the news was good for the more economically robust Việt Nam because serious social challenges accompanied these new economic gains.

Economic Good Times

At a December 1986 Việt Nam Communist Party (VCP) meeting, younger and less doctrinaire party members, who were not wedded to socialism as an economic system, pushed through a new policy called Đổi mới (Economic Renovation). The experiment was to attempt a market-driven economy while maintaining a socialist political system. An aspect of Đổi mới included a surprising reform allowing relatively unrestricted foreign investment in the Vietnamese economy. Compared to other Southeast Asian countries, anthropology professor Hy V. Luong perhaps best described the changes: "[T]his was a very liberal law, allowing for 100 percent foreign ownership and profit repatriation, significant tax holidays, and concessions of enterprises investing in a number of priority areas (including exports, consumer goods, technology transfer, and processing of local raw materials)."[1] There was no immediate international response to Việt Nam's invitation to foreign investors. The United States still did not have normal relations with Việt Nam, and the international community disapproved of Việt Nam's continued occupation of Cambodia. Still, Việt Nam slowly advanced its economic reforms between 1986 and 1988. By 1988 Việt Nam's inflation rate had reached 1000 percent. That same year a famine in northern Việt Nam was so severe that SRV officials privately appealed for help from allied communist states. But 1988 would be the end of Việt Nam's economic desperation. The Vietnamese Politburo issued Resolution 10, which ended widespread collectivization of land and labor. The following year Việt Nam withdrew its forces from Cambodia, ending a costly ten-year occupation.

The breakup of Việt Nam's state-run collectives fundamentally changed SRV society. First, not only did the state withdraw from its day-to-day management of people's lives but it also abandoned the two-tier pricing system. Instead the state followed market rates rather than the irrational, lower, government-controlled prices. Land also changed hands. Individuals were allowed to buy fifteen-year leases on property; furthermore, farmers began developing their "own" land using more modern technologies for increasing rice harvests. One consequence of farm privatization was that Việt Nam saw its national rice production move from twelve million tons in 1988 to thirty-eight million in 2009. This increase helped to jump-start Việt Nam's economy. Farmers were now able to follow their agrarian passions in the rice paddies. As one writer noted in 1995, "As for the farmers, who still make up three-quarters of Việt Nam's 73.5 million people, their overriding concern is the same as it has been for 2000 years: to plant the next rice harvest."[2]

As the state loosened its economic grip on the country, the ingenuity, hard work, and determined character of the farmers moved Việt Nam away from starvation and toward its position as a major global supplier of various commodities. The introduction of new fertilizers and strains of rice seedlings increased the yields of rice from 1.83 tons per hectare in 1975 to 5.23 tons per hectare in 2008. But Việt Nam's economic boom brought new challenges for millions within the country.

An obvious consequence of more private property and agricultural output was that land values rose dramatically. For example, a hectare of paddy land along the national highway sold for around thirty thousand dollars in 1991; ten years later that same land was worth more than one hundred thousand dollars![3] Escalating land prices attracted speculators, who began buying and selling significant amounts of property. Caught in this whirlwind of a new economic paradigm, farmers found themselves torn between their love of land and the promise of quick money to be made

Figure 9.1. A typical scene in one of Việt Nam's most crowded places, Hồ Chí Minh City. Urbanization has transformed twenty-first-century Việt Nam. (Courtesy of Margrethe Store, http://commons.wikimedia.org/wiki/File:Ho_Chi_Minh_City_street_2.jpg.)

by selling leases to investors. Robert Templer, the author of an influential work on modern Việt Nam, rightly concludes, "After years of socialist controls, the freedom to use, purchase, rent, inherit or sell land set in motion the gears of speculation, and slowly the attendant wheels of elation and fear began to turn. Land has again become almost everything, a source not just of wealth but of identity. . . . Property developers appeared out of nowhere. Plaster and pilasters went up in an orgy of architectural excess and a low fog of scandal and deceit settled over the city."[4]

Even with their newly acquired farm leases, farmers remain somewhat at the mercy of the government because it still sets the price floor for rice to reportedly save farmers from the vagaries of the volatile global market. But while the set price is often reasonable compared to international prices, farmers also have to pay broker fees and so lose out on the profits the state garners by reselling Việt Nam's white gold. So, while farmers have moved beyond subsistence farming, they do not receive the significant benefits from Việt Nam's engagement in the international market. To be sure, rural Vietnamese have grown wealthier since 1989, but corruption is endemic among SRV officials, who often control permits for new businesses, real estate deals, and access to an open market system.

After the 1986 economic reforms, rice was only one of several commodities Vietnamese farmers began growing for export purposes. In 1990 they produced 92,000 tons of coffee; ten years later, coffee production totaled 698,000 tons. Again land use proved to be a bit of a problem as the ground used for growing coffee increased from 119,000 hectares in 1992 to 516,000 in 2002. Farmers continued to complain that the government still overregulated what could be grown on farms. Author Robert Templer notes that the government's "insistence of making people grow rice diverts labour and capital away from more lucrative activities and does little to ensure food security."[5] Yet, even as farmers are allowed to use land for commercial agriculture, they are betting on unstable global market prices. For example, Vietnamese entrepreneurs who jumped on the coffee-growing bandwagon watched the world price of coffee dive from 4,000 dollars a ton in 1994 to 320 dollars a ton in 2001!

As land has increased in value following decollectivization, lowland farmers and entrepreneurs have rushed into Việt Nam's central highlands to lease prime farmland for use in commercial agriculture. These lands are home to indigenous ethnic minorities who at times have been pushed aside in the wake of new national economic opportunities about which they know very little. For example, while Vietnamese farmers, officials, and middlemen reaped great benefits from the highlands' soil, a 1997 study cited by the Harvard-trained anthropologist Hy V. Luong indicated that in Việt Nam's central highlands' Dalak province twenty-two of twenty-nine ethnic minority communities did not have enough food to survive. And while Việt Nam prospered, the 1992 recorded poverty rate among its highlanders stood at 86 percent.[6]

A final note about land and farmers: some Vietnamese still lived in collectives even after the 1988 law allowed farmers to lease their own land, and they protested against state corruption. Government officials took advantage of farmers who worked in collectives in order to maintain their privileged lives. As time passed these farmers viewed their situation as regressive compared to that of their peers who leased their own land. During the early 1990s, thousands of collective farmers began attacking government offices and the officials themselves, insisting on fundamental changes to bring communes up to the same economic standards as farms on leased land. As the remaining collectives slowly faded into economic irrelevance, so, too, did many other state-owned enterprises. State industrial cooperatives decreased in number from 32,034 in 1988 to 949 in 1998; individuals working in state industrial cooperatives decreased from 1,117,800 to 76,274 during that same decade. This economic vacuum

Figure 9.2. Hồ Chí Minh City's Bitexco Financial Tower, one
of the many new high-rise commercial buildings in the rapidly
expanding city. (Courtesy of Felix Triller, http://commons.
wikimedia.org/wiki/File:Bitexco_Financial_Tower,_Ho_Chi_
Minh_City,_Vietnam.jpg.)

was filled by private enterprise. Between 1988 and 1998 in Việt Nam,
private businesses increased in number from 318 to 5,714, and the number
of workers in private household businesses jumped from 923,000 to
1,847,777.[7] Obviously, farmland wasn't the only thing becoming private
in Việt Nam.

While Việt Nam's overall economic situation dramatically improved
following decollectivization and the Đổi mới policies, its growth has been
uneven, causing jealousies and significant internal migration. In particular
HCMC has once again become the center of economic activity just as it

had been during the RVN era. With a population well over seven million, commercial real estate in downtown Sài Gòn (as most Vietnamese still refer to HCMC) is some of the most expensive in the world. By the late 1990s southeastern Việt Nam—with only 13 percent of the country's population—accounted for almost a third of the nation's economy. Like other Southeast Asian countries, Việt Nam will need to address the disparity of wealth between the city and the countryside.

SOCIETY AND CHANGES

The VCP leadership is trying to manage the country's economic prosperity without losing its grip on society, as the country seems to be changing just as rapidly and dramatically as the price of real estate. While the government tries to control social change, Vietnamese are now as plugged into global popular culture as rice brokers are into world trade. One example of a modern social crisis the SRV is trying to solve is the spread of HIV/AIDS. In 2010 more than a quarter million Vietnamese were HIV-positive, with fourteen thousand having died the previous year due to AIDS.

Initially Vietnamese were told that HIV was a disease from which only foreigners suffered. But the government has gradually realized the need to educate its population about the way the disease is contracted. Officials have also reluctantly allowed international nongovernmental organizations (NGOs) to join in working with AIDS patients. Even religious institutions are permitted to conduct mercy ministries among those on the margins of society who are most likely to suffer from sexually transmitted diseases and mental illness. These NGOs are particularly needed in twenty-first-century Việt Nam for four reasons: increasing societal alienation, attitudes toward sex, the cost of health care, and the increasing irrelevance of the government.

While Việt Nam's economic transformation has helped millions, it has also led to a cultural crisis for many. For example, the vast majority of Vietnamese born after 1975 consider war veterans insignificant. People who are either too busy for or indifferent to the veterans' patriotic service fail to give them the honor they deserve. Thousands of veterans trudge through urban parks looking for something to give meaning to their past service and present despair. Often their search leads them to old decrepit villas where they join young men and women who are turning to heroin to escape their own boredom and depression. Urban youths who are too poor to own the shiny motor scooters that identify the success of young professionals also seek meaning in destructive, socially alienating

Figure 9.3. Vietnamese women at Sài Gòn University, established in 2007. The *ao dai* is the traditional dress for Vietnamese women. (US public domain.)

activities such as gang fighting. Drug use among these disenfranchised urban dwellers also contributes to the spread of HIV in Việt Nam.

Heterosexual activity is the main vehicle for the spread of AIDS in Việt Nam. In particular, prostitution is an acceptable profession among many Vietnamese as daughters fulfill their supportive obligations to their families by moving to cities to work in bars, massage parlors, and other sex-service establishments. One observer notes, "Prostitution is acceptable as part of the sacrifices women must make for their families. . . . Visiting prostitutes is part of male bonding and growing up; it marks a transition from adolescence to adulthood. Paying for sex is not the furtive, hidden pursuit that it has become in the West, but a social activity, often done with friends."[8]

An estimated six hundred thousand sex workers are scattered throughout Việt Nam, and government speeches about the need to live for the state have not stopped the spread of HIV. A symbol of the state's acknowledgment of the problem is its encouragement of the wide distribution of condoms to stave off a disaster such as the one now occurring in neighboring Thailand.

Việt Nam's market economy has also shifted the cost of health care from the state to the individual. In 1992–93, the state only met 16 percent of the country's health care costs. Today if a person is ill in Việt Nam they must use their own resources to pay for a doctor's visit or hospital stay. Professor Luong notes that an operation now costs "the equivalent of one year of income for a relatively poor rural family."[9] Since HIV/AIDS patients are in need of specialized medicines, the state now accepts foreign support to help treat the ill.

CONCLUSION

Writing in 1995, one SRV observer noted that "the communist leaders have had no real choice but to open the country to the outside world and hope that they can subdue the forces thereby unleashed."[10] If one of Việt Nam's "unleashed" social forces is urban youths strung out on heroin and suffering from HIV or AIDS, a possible positive consequence of this is that the SRV has opened its door to international organizations to help alleviate Việt Nam's social problems.

Finally, observers note that while Vietnamese are willing to live within the confines of the authoritarian rule of the VCP, they have very little passion for, or confidence in, their government. David Marr and Christine White, outstanding scholars of Việt Nam, observed that by 1986 "the majority of citizens had lost confidence in the existing leadership."[11] Economic prosperity has not done anything to inspire greater affection for SRV officials. The party struggles to attract young members; moreover, in 1996 less than 1.7 percent of HCMC's five million citizens were party members, which illustrates the continued apathy toward the SRV government. My Linh, a Vietnamese popular singer, frankly stated, "The party is completely irrelevant to me and my friends. I'm sure they would like to use me (to promote the party to young people). But why should I join? The party does nothing for my career or for other artists. We don't need it."[12]

According to many Vietnamese, the reason for their apathy toward the government is its well-deserved reputation for corruption. Occasionally the government will turn on one of its own to make a public show of punishing a corrupt official, but the pervasive need to bribe officials at all levels has cast a shadow over a culture that once valued relationships more than immediate payment for services.

According to an old saying, there are two tragic things in life: not getting what you hope for and getting what you hope for. Government officials wanted to pull Việt Nam out of the downward spiral of a failed state-controlled economy. By allowing private enterprise, they were successful—perhaps even beyond their wildest dreams. But accompanying this prosperity is a society filled with spiritual, emotional, and identity struggles of quiet desperation. And it is uncertain whether the party can provide adequate answers to its citizens.

10

CONCLUSION

Việt Nam is often associated with war. Chinese, Mongol, Japanese, Cham, French, and American armies are intertwined with Việt Nam's history because of armed conflict on Vietnamese soil. But Việt Nam's military past is only one dimension of its multifaceted history. It is best to look at Việt Nam's past and present as one views the world—through the interwoven colors of a spectrum. There are innumerable threads of time, values, and lives that make up the beautiful tapestry we call Việt Nam.

From the outset of Vietnamese civilization, three forces outside its control shaped how its history would unfold: Chinese civilization, the seacoast, and rainfall. Even before the Common Era, significant aspects of Vietnamese culture, such as writing, art, religion, political systems, and philosophy, were heavily guided by Chinese thought and institutions that predated Việt Nam. Based on its size, geographic proximity, ancient roots, and cultural sophistication, China significantly helped to mold Việt Nam.

A second influence on Việt Nam is the South China Sea. The lengthy two-thousand-mile coastline constitutes the entire eastern border of Việt Nam's north-south landmass. Consequently, the outside world was always quite accessible to the Vietnamese. From across the world, religions such as Buddhism and Christianity were brought to Việt Nam's doorstep by missionaries and traders who used the oceans and seas as highways and ships as vehicles. The South China Sea also served as an open door to trade with the early kingdoms of Southeast Asia's archipelagos. This international interaction kept Việt Nam plugged into a world much larger than itself.

The third prehistorical influence on Việt Nam is rain. All of Việt Nam receives substantial amounts of rain—some areas as much as 120 inches per year. The Vietnamese response to such annual torrents provides a window into their character. Following the rhythms of wet and dry seasons, Vietnamese used their time to do the hard work of planting, nurturing, and harvesting the life-sustaining grain of rice. This meant that the primary way to get ahead in life—if not even just to survive—was the backbreaking work of planting rice. Well-known Canadian author and journalist Malcolm Gladwell perhaps put it best when he wrote, "Throughout history, not surprisingly, the people who grow rice have always worked harder than almost any other kind of farmer."[1] Commitment to the grueling labor of farming helps to explain the determined character of the Vietnamese.

But civilizations don't often choose neighbors or climate. While the three forces noted above influenced Vietnamese society, they did not define what it means to be Vietnamese. Despite China's influence, and even its political incorporation of Việt Nam into its empires for a millennium, the Vietnamese do not speak Chinese, their food is distinctive, and basic Vietnamese social relations and values differ from those of the Chinese. The persistent regard for their unique culture despite centuries of foreign rule testifies to the strength and depth of the Vietnamese people.

Although given its eastern seacoast Việt Nam was vulnerable to invasion and occupation, the Vietnamese have thus far avoided permanent subjugation to external powers. To be sure multiple empires and nations used the waters around Việt Nam to bring massive naval forces close to Vietnamese territory and have even shelled its coastal towns. Yet Việt Nam remains independent while many of these foreign vessels are part of the dustheap of history.

Given such a history and the depth of character of its peoples, one might think that Việt Nam's future appears rather secure. Certainly its record of overcoming external threats and internal divisions is impressive. But Việt Nam's story is a dynamic narrative with old and new challenges to be faced. For example, in 2011 China became the world's second-leading economy, having passed Japan while gaining ground on the United States. Việt Nam will once again have to adjust its foreign policy priorities based on the meteoric economic and military rise of its historic northern adversary. It was only as recently as 1979 that China invaded Việt Nam, and the PRC's armed forces are, because of massive military spending, much more powerful today. For its part China seeks peace in Southeast Asia, but it also expects respect—if not deference—from its former tributary states. Việt Nam will have to come to terms with these new geopolitical realities.

Việt Nam's greatest current challenge is internal. After enduring centuries of military, political, and economic chaos, how will the Vietnamese respond to relative peace and prosperity? Life was less complicated for the Vietnamese when everyone was poor and struggling against the threat of tyranny. Higher living standards are currently possible, but technology and hyperglobalization pose challenges for Vietnamese society. Younger people, particularly residents of urban areas, are in constant contact with other cultures whose values contradict traditional indigenous cultural principles. Now the Vietnamese must answer the hard questions about what is more important: family or wealth, spirituality or entertainment, individualism or community, opportunity or loyalty, modernity or tradition, unbridled economic growth or the environment, information or wisdom, state control or freedom. These questions are at the heart of twenty-first-century Việt Nam. How the Vietnamese respond to such matters will largely determine the unfolding of the next chapter in their long, rich, and varied national narrative.

NOTES

CHAPTER 1

[1] Neil L. Jamieson, *Understanding Vietnam* (Los Angeles: University of California Press, 1993), 6.

CHAPTER 2

[1] Maitrii Aung-Thwin et al., *A New History of Southeast Asia* (New York: Palgrave Macmillan, 2010), 24.

[2] Keith Weller Taylor, *The Birth of Vietnam* (Los Angeles: University of California Press, 1983), 76.

[3] Ibid., 53.

[4] J. C. van Leur, *Indonesian Trade and Society: Essays in Asian Social and Economic History* (Dordrecht, Netherlands: Foris Publications, 1983).

CHAPTER 3

[1] Neil L. Jamieson, *Understanding Vietnam* (Los Angeles: University of California Press, 1993), 9.

[2] An excellent overview of the different notions of power in Southeast Asia is found in Benedict Anderson, "The Idea of Power in Javanese Culture," in *Culture and Politics in Indonesia*, ed. Claire Holt (Ithaca, NY: Cornell University Press, 1972).

[3] For a solid introduction to the Mongol empire, see J. McIver Weatherford, *Genghis Khan and the Making of the Modern World* (New York: Crown, 2004).

[4] Keith Taylor, "The Early Kingdoms," in *The Cambridge History of Southeast Asia*, vol. 1, pt. 1: *From Early Times to c. 1500*, ed. Nicholas Tarling (New York: Cambridge University Press, 1992), 149.

[5] Roland Jacques, *Portuguese Pioneers of Vietnamese Linguistics prior to 1650* (Bangkok: Orchid Press, 2002).

[6] This religious pluralism is explained in Tài Thu' Nguyễn and Thi Tho' Hoàng, *The History of Buddhism in Vietnam* (Washington, DC: Council for Research in

Values and Philosophy, Institute of Philosophy, Vietnamese Academy of Social Sciences, 2008).

CHAPTER 4

[1] For more on the Ming fleet, see Louise Levathes, *When China Ruled the Seas: The Treasure Fleet of the Dragon Throne, 1405–1433* (New York: Oxford University Press, 1996).

[2] George Dutton, "A Brief History of the Tayson Movement (1771–1802)," http://www.vietspring.org/history/tayson.html.

[3] Maitrii Aung-Thwin et al., *A New History of Southeast Asia* (New York: Palgrave Macmillan, 2010), 146.

CHAPTER 5

[1] Rudyard Kipling, "The White Man's Burden" in *The Global Experience: Readings in World History since 1850*, eds. Philip F. Riley, et al. (New Jersey: Prentice-Hall, Inc., 1970), 135–36. This poem was written to America when the United States took possession of the Philippines following the 1898 Spanish American War.

[2] The ten colonized Southeast Asia countries and their former rulers are Burma, Singapore, Malaysia, and Brunei (Great Britain); the Philippines (Spain and the United States); Vietnam, Laos, and Cambodia (France); Indonesia (the Netherlands); and East Timor (Portugal).

[3] Neil L. Jamieson, *Understanding Vietnam* (Los Angeles: University of California Press, 1993), 43.

[4] William J. Duiker, *Ho Chi Minh* (New York: Hyperion, 2000), 62.

[5] John W. Dower, *Embracing Defeat: Japan in the Wake of World War II* (New York: W. W. Norton, 1999), 36.

[6] Duiker, *Ho Chi Minh*, 323.

CHAPTER 6

[1] Elizabeth Deane, *Vietnam: A Television History*, vol. 2: *America's Mandarin*, http://karws.gso.uri.edu/Marsh/Việt Nam/103ts.html.

CHAPTER 7

[1] Frederick Z. Brown, "Vietnam since the War (1975–1995)," *Wilson Quarterly* 19, no. 1 (1995): 66.

[2] Ibid., 76–77.

[3] David G. Marr et al., eds., *Postwar Vietnam: Dilemmas in Socialist Development* (Ithaca, NY: Southeast Asia Program, Cornell University, 1988), 1.

[4] Ibid., 2.

[5] Ibid., 3.

[6] Ken MacLean, "The Rehabilitation of an Uncomfortable Past: Everyday Life in Vietnam during the Subsidy Period (1975–1986)," *History and Anthropology* 19, no. 3 (2008): 282.

[7] Brown, "Vietnam since the War," 77.

[8] MacLean, "Rehabilitation of an Uncomfortable Past," 283.

[9] Ng Shui Meng, "Vietnam in 1983: Keeping a Delicate Balance," in *Southeast Asian Affairs,* ed. Pushpa Thambipillai (Singapore: ISEAS, 1984): 352.

[10] MacLean, "Rehabilitation of an Uncomfortable Past," 296.

[11] Marr et al., *Postwar Vietnam*, 4.

[12] Brown, "Vietnam since the War," 77.

CHAPTER 9

[1] Hy V. Luong, *Postwar Vietnam: Dynamics of a Transforming Society* (Lanham, MD: Institute of Southeast Asian Studies and Rowman & Littlefield, 2003), 16.

[2] Frederick Z. Brown, "Vietnam since the War (1975–1995)," *Wilson Quarterly* 19, no. 1 (1995): 65.

[3] Luong, *Postwar Vietnam*, 3.

[4] Robert Templer, *Shadows and Wind: A View of Modern Vietnam* (New York: Penguin Books, 1999), 205.

[5] Ibid., 61.

[6] Luong, *Postwar Vietnam*, 8.

[7] Ibid., 3.

[8] Templer, *Shadows and Wind: A View of Modern Vietnam*, 244–45.

[9] Luong, *Postwar Vietnam*, 6.

[10] Brown, "Vietnam since the War," 65.

[11] David G. Marr et al., eds., *Postwar Vietnam: Dilemmas in Socialist Development* (Ithaca, NY: Southeast Asia Program, Cornell University, 1988), 4–5.

[12] Mark McDonald, "Vietnam's Communist Party Struggles to Attract Youths," *San Jose Mercury News*, February 6, 2000.

CHAPTER 10

[1] Malcolm Gladwell, *Outliers: The Story of Success* (New York: Little, Brown, 2008), 233.

Glossary

ARVN: The Army of the Republic of Việt Nam, the South Vietnamese armed forces supported by the United States to help the Republic of Việt Nam fend off threats from internal and external communist forces.

Bạch Đằng River: River that flows into the Gulf of Tonkin, where Vietnamese placed iron and bamboo spikes just below the surface of the water, which served to entrap Chinese and Mongol naval invasion forces during the tenth and thirteenth centuries.

Cao Đài: A religious movement that started in 1919 in southern Việt Nam. The faith incorporated elements of Buddhism, Confucianism, Islam, Christianity, and Daoism.

Champa: An ancient kingdom formed in what is now Cambodia. At various times, Champa served as both an ally and an enemy of the earliest Vietnamese dynasties.

Confucianism: A Chinese philosophy that emphasizes the importance of ritual, relationships, and cultivating the mind.

de Behaine, Pigneau: An eighteenth-century French priest who was instrumental in supporting Prince Anh's quest to unite Việt Nam.

de Rhodes, Alexander: The seventeenth-century French priest who created Quốc Ngữ, a romanized system for writing Vietnamese.

Điện Biên Phủ, Battle of: Battle between the Việt Minh and French on the border of Laos and Việt Nam, which resulted in the worst defeat for France in its imperial history.

Đổi mới: Policy, meaning "renovation," that was implemented in Việt Nam during 1986 with the intention of moving the country away from a strictly state-controlled economy.

DRV: The Democratic Republic of Việt Nam, established by Hồ Chí Minh and his colleagues in 1945. After the 1954 Geneva Conference, the DRV encompassed Việt Nam's territory north of the seventeenth parallel.

Geneva Conference: The 1954 international gathering of diplomats who met to try and find a solution to the French-Vietnamese War, which was in its eighth year. The final agreement included the provision that Việt Nam would be divided at the seventeenth parallel, and a plebiscite was scheduled for 1956 so the Vietnamese could decide their future. The plebiscite did not take place, and the divided Việt Nam led to the American–Việt Nam War.

Gia Long: The name Prince Anh gave himself at the turn of the nineteenth century. He founded Việt Nam's last dynasty, the Nguyễn (1802–1945).

Hồ Chí Minh: Man who became the face of the communist movement in Việt Nam. His time in France, Russia, and China helped him create a network of international communist movements. Although he was absent from Việt Nam for three decades, his reputation as a patriot and leader actually grew during his absence. He declared the independence of Việt Nam on September 2, 1945.

Hòa Hảo: Religion founded in 1939 by a Vietnamese mystic named Huỳnh Phú Sổ. Hòa Hảo combined elements of Buddhism and folk religion with a message of social justice. After World War II, Hòa Hảo leaders supported the return of French rule in southern Việt Nam.

Huế: An urban center in central Việt Nam, which became the imperial capital during Việt Nam's last dynasty, the Nguyễn (1802–1945).

Indochina Union: The political system that helped the French control Việt Nam, Cambodia, and Laos. Created in 1887, the union included Cambodia, Tonkin, and Annam as protectorates and Cochinchina as a colony. Laos was added as a protectorate in 1893.

Khmer Rouge: The name given to Cambodian communists who stayed in Cambodia despite orders to leave the country in 1954. The movement eventually gained enough strength to overthrow the pro-American Cambodian government in 1975.

Lê dynasty: Dynasty (1428–1788) that started out strong, having defeated occupying Chinese forces, but was eventually dominated by Vietnamese military and aristocratic clans. It was founded by Lê Lợi (1384–1433).

Lý dynasty: The first independent Vietnamese dynasty (1009–1225) following China's thousand-year rule over Việt Nam. The Buddhist church helped to establish its founder, Lý Cong Uan (974–1028), as the paramount leader in Việt Nam.

Ngô Đình Diệm: Leader of the Republic of Việt Nam from 1955 to 1963. While he was initially supported by the United States, he lost the support of many American officials and was assassinated in 1963.

Nguyễn dynasty: Việt Nam's last dynasty (1802–1945). It was during this dynasty that Việt Nam was divided and ruled by France.

NLF: National Liberation Front, the South Vietnamese organization that opposed the pro-American RVN government. The NLF used political and military means to disrupt the South Vietnamese government.

SRV: Socialist Republic of Việt Nam, the name given to the reunited Việt Nam in 1976.

Tây Sơn Rebellion: Uprising led by three brothers from Nghĩa Bình province in 1771. The rebels sought to alleviate growing exploitation by the rich landowning class. Initial successes gave way to internal and external fighting, which ended with the rebels' defeat at the hands of the French-backed Prince Anh.

Tết Offensive: Multiple attacks on the ARVN and Americans in South Việt Nam launched during the Vietnamese New Year celebration in 1968. While the offensive was a military failure, it was a political success as more Americans began to question the US role in Việt Nam.

Việt cộng: Pejorative term given to southern Vietnamese who opposed the policies and rule of the pro-American officials of the Republic of Việt Nam. They fought the pro-American ARVN and were supported by North Việt Nam.

Việt Minh: Organization formed during World War II to defeat occupying Japanese soldiers and alleviate the suffering of poor Vietnamese peasants. While it was initially supported by the United States, the Việt Minh eventually fought the French and Americans who were occupying Việt Nam.

VNQDD: The Vietnamese Nationalist Party founded in 1927. Its leaders patterned their organization after the Chinese Nationalist Party. The VNQDD provided an ideological alternative to the Indochinese Communist Party. It suffered from a lack of funds and a failed uprising in 1930.

SUGGESTIONS FOR FURTHER READING

Aung-Thwin, Maitrii, M. C. Rickleffs, Bruce Lockhart, Albert Lau, and Portia Reyes. *A New History of Southeast Asia*. New York: Palgrave Macmillan, 2010.

Brown, Frederick Z. "Vietnam since the War (1975–1995)." *Wilson Quarterly* 19, no. 1 (1995): 64–87.

Chapuis, Oscar. *A History of Vietnam: From Hong Bang to Tu Duc*. Westport, CT: Greenwood Press, 1995.

Duiker, William J. *Ho Chi Minh*. New York: Hyperion, 2000.

Dutton, George Edson. *The Tây Son Uprising: Society and Rebellion in Eighteenth-Century Vietnam*. Honolulu: University of Hawai'i Press, 2006.

Epstein, Mitch. *Vietnam: A Book of Changes*. New York: Center for Documentary Studies in association with W. W. Norton, 1997.

Fforde, Adam, and Stefan De Vylder. *From Plan to Market: The Economic Transition in Vietnam*. Boulder, CO: Westview Press, 1996.

Halberstam, David. *The Making of a Quagmire: America and Việt Nam during the Kennedy Era*. New York: Random House, 1965.

Hayslip, Le Ly, and Jay Wurts. *When Heaven and Earth Changed Places: A Vietnamese Woman's Journey from War to Peace*. New York: Doubleday, 1989.

Herring, George C. *America's Longest War: The United States and Vietnam, 1950–1975*. Boston: McGraw-Hill, 2002.

Jacques, Roland. *Portuguese Pioneers of Vietnamese Linguistics Prior to 1650*. Bangkok: Orchid Press, 2002.

Jamieson, Neil L. *Understanding Vietnam*. Los Angeles: University of California Press, 1993.

Karnow, Stanley. *Vietnam: A History*. New York: Viking Press, 1983.

Kerkvliet, Benedict J., and Doug J. Porter. *Vietnam's Rural Transformation*. Boulder, CO: Westview Press, 1995.

Kolko, Gabriel. *Vietnam: Anatomy of a Peace*. New York: Routledge, 1997.

Lockhart, Bruce McFarland. *The End of the Vietnamese Monarchy*. New Haven, CT: Council on Southeast Asia Studies, Yale University, 1993.

Lockhart, Bruce McFarland, and William J. Duiker. *Historical Dictionary of Vietnam*. Lanham, MD: Scarecrow Press, 2006.

Luong, Hy V. *Postwar Vietnam: Dynamics of a Transforming Society*. Lanham, MD.: Institute of Southeast Asian Studies and Rowman & Littlefield, 2003.

MacLean, Ken. "The Rehabilitation of an Uncomfortable Past: Everyday Life in Vietnam during the Subsidy Period (1975–1986)." *History and Anthropology* 19, no. 3 (2008): 281–303.

Malarney, Shaun. *Culture, Ritual, and Revolution in Vietnam*. Richmond, VA: Curzon, 2001.

Marr, David G. *Vietnamese Tradition on Trial, 1920–1945*. Berkeley: University of California Press, 1981.

Marr, David G., Christine Pelzer White, eds. *Postwar Vietnam: Dilemmas in Socialist Development*. Ithaca, NY: Southeast Asia Program, Cornell University, 1988.

McLeod, Mark W. *The Vietnamese Response to French Intervention, 1862–1874*. New York: Praeger, 1991.

Meng, Ng Shui. "Vietnam in 1983: Keeping a Delicate Balance" in *Southeast Asian Affairs* (1984), edited by Pushpa Thambipilla. Singapore: ISEAS, 1984: 343–68.

Ngô, Vinh Long. *Before the Revolution: The Vietnamese Peasants under the French*. Cambridge, MA: MIT Press, 1973.

Nguyễn, Tài Thu' and Thi Tho' Hoàng. *The History of Buddhism in Vietnam*. Washington, DC: Council for Research in Values and Philosophy, Institute of Philosophy, Vietnamese Academy of Social Sciences, 2008.

Pham, Andrew X. *Catfish and Mandala: A Two-Wheeled Voyage through the Landscape and Memory of Vietnam*. New York: Farrar, Straus and Giroux, 1999.

———. *The Eaves of Heaven: A Life in Three Wars*. New York: Harmony Books, 2008.

Porter, Gareth. *Vietnam: The Politics of Bureaucratic Socialism*. Ithaca, NY: Cornell University Press, 1993.

Ratliff, William E. *Vietnam Rising: Culture and Change in Asia's Tiger Cub*. Oakland, CA: Independent Institute, 2008.

Shawcross, William. *The Quality of Mercy: Cambodia, Holocaust, and Modern Conscience*. New York: Simon and Schuster, 1984.

Taylor, Keith Weller. *The Birth of Vietnam*. Los Angeles: University of California Press, 1983.

———. "The Early Kingdoms." In *The Cambridge History of Southeast Asia*. Vol. 1, pt. 1: *From Early Times to c. 1500*, edited by Nicholas Tarling. New York: Cambridge University Press, 1992.

Templer, Robert. *Shadows and Wind: A View of Modern Vietnam*. New York: Penguin Books, 1999.

Tran-Nam, Binh, and Chi Do Pham. *The Vietnamese Economy: Awakening the Dormant Dragon*. New York: Routledge, 2003.

Tru'o'ng, Nhu' Tang, David Chanoff, and Van Toai Doan. *A Vietcong Memoir*. San Diego: Harcourt Brace Jovanovich, 1985.

Turley, William S., and Mark Selden. *Reinventing Vietnamese Socialism: Doi Moi in Comparative Perspective*. Boulder, CO: Westview Press, 1993.

Werner, Jayne Susan. *Peasant Politics and Religious Sectarianism: Peasant and Priest in the Cao Dai in Việt Nam*. New Haven, CT: Council on Southeast Asia Studies, Yale University, 1981.

Williams, Michael C. *Vietnam at the Crossroads*. New York: Council on Foreign Relations Press, 1992.

Woodside, Alexander. *Vietnam and the Chinese Model: A Comparative Study of Nguyen and Chi'ng Civil Government in the First Half of the Nineteenth Century*. Cambridge, MA: Harvard University Press, 1971.